URBAN TRANSIT POLICY
An Economic and Political History

DAVID W. JONES, JR.

University of California, Berkeley

PRENTICE-HALL, INC., Englewood Cliffs, New Jersey 07632

Library of Congress Cataloging in Publication Data

Jones, David W. (date)
   Urban transit policy.

   Includes bibliographies and index.
   1. Local transit–Government policy–United States--
History. 2. Federal aid to transportation--United
States–History. 3. Local transit–United States--
History. I. Title.
HE4461.J66 1985   388.4'068   84-17703
ISBN 0-13-939257-2

388.4
J 76 u

MLA

Cover design: *Lundgren Graphics, Ltd.*
Manufacturing buyer: *Anthony Caruso*

Printed in the United States of America

10 9 8 7 6 5 4 3 2 1

ISBN 0-13-939257-2   01

Prentice-Hall International, Inc., *London*
Prentice-Hall of Australia Pty. Limited, *Sydney*
Editora Prentice-Hall do Brasil, Ltda., *Rio de Janeiro*
Prentice-Hall Canada Inc., *Toronto*
Prentice-Hall of India Private Limited, *New Delhi*
Prentice-Hall of Japan, Inc., *Tokyo*
Prentice-Hall of Southeast Asia Pte. Ltd., *Singapore*
Whitehall Books Limited, *Wellington, New Zealand*

CONTENTS

ACKNOWLEDGMENTS

This book is the product of a two-year sabbatical in residence at the Institute of Transportation Studies, University of California, Berkeley. The Institute not only paid my salary, but also provided research and clerical assistance, and a forum for testing and refining ideas. The book would not have been possible without ITS support and the generosity of ITS Director, Adib Kanafani.

Much of the research for this book was conducted in the stacks and attic of the ITS library. Librarians Catherine Cortelyou and Michael Kleiber spent hours combing through their extraordinary collection and retrieving fugitive publications. Their personal interest in the project and their tolerance of my endless requests were above and beyond the call of duty.

Many other debts are owed. To Bill Garrison whose very presence in the office next door sets demanding standards of intellectual effort. To Marty Wachs of UCLA whose thoughtful criticism of an early draft propelled a multitude of revisions. To Jane Clayton and Jonathan Gifford—students who were as quick to teach as to learn. To five masters of transportation with whom I have apprenticed over the years: Bill Schaefer and Gene Hardin of the California Department of Transportation; Paul Bay of Portland's Tri-Met Transit Authority; Milt Brooks of the Urban Mass Transportation Administration; and Dick Shevell of Stanford University. To all of them, I owe an enormous intellectual debt.

Finally, there is another more important debt that is owed: To my wife, Inta and our children, Kristin and Katie. I love them very much.

PREFACE

Different people think about policy in different ways and thus have very different views of what constitutes sound and effective policy. This book examines a particular public policy—transit policy in the United States—from a historical perspective. The perspective of history is useful because it reminds us that policy is a changeable and changing social contract created by negotiation among parties at interest. This social contract steers how organizations conduct their day-to-day operations, how they use technology and expertise, and how they are able to use labor and capital.

Transit policy is a social contract in which many parties have a stake and an interest: the transit rider, the transit worker, the taxpayer, the downtown employer, the motorist, just to name a few. It is a complicated contract that has been renegotiated many times since horse-drawn transit systems were first chartered in the 19th century. The operative word here is *negotiated*. Policy is negotiated, not formulated.

Renegotiating policy is both necessary and difficult. It is difficult because renegotiation upsets established ways of doing things and threatens interests vested in previous rounds of negotiation. Parties with a stake in the status quo are prone to resist renegotiation; they would prefer stable policy, a static contract—a surer thing.

Nonetheless, the renegotiation of policy is necessary because economic conditions, technological opportunities, and social aspirations change. Sure and steady may describe sound policy over the short run, but over longer periods of time, good policy is dynamic, responsive and evolutionary. Thus, policy is *necessarily* a sometime thing. It is a contract that *must* be amended and renegotiated. Policies that aren't dynamic and responsive eventually chafe against changed social conditions and changing opportunities. They bind rather than serve.

There is an important and potentially problematic difference between policies that are good for the short run and those that are good for the long run. The difference is particularly important in a society where change is rapid and organizations are large. Large organizations rely on routinization and standardization to achieve efficiencies and economies of scale. But, over the long run, routinization and standardization may harden into inertia and inflexibility. What once contributed to efficiency may later contribute to obsolescence. The dilemma is a general one in modern society; transit policy represents a special case.

Many authors who have written about transit policy in the United States have characterized it as erratic and volatile. Public policy has veered and turned, it is said, in a fashion that has made sound investment and efficient management difficult in the extreme. This is true. American transit policy has been neither sure nor steady. Paradoxically, however, the most difficult transit policy problem in the United States is not volatility, but rather inertia and deadlock. Change in the transit industry has not paced change in economic conditions, technological opportunities and social aspirations. American cities have changed profoundly since transit was the dominant means of urban transportation, while transit systems have changed relatively little. This is because the transit industry operates with an enormous burden of traditions and routines—policies that are deeply imbedded, and thus hidden, in its institutional structure, in its routing and scheduling procedures, in its fleet mix, in its fare and route structures, and in its labor agreements.

The routines, traditions and working agreements of an industry constitute its most basic policies. These policies condition what kind of technology it can use, how it puts technology and people together into operations, and what markets it can serve effectively and efficiently. Policies that become imbedded as routines and traditions are not always recognized as policies—or even as choices that preclude what might be better alternatives. *Imbedded* policies have a way of becoming "our way of doing business." They are taken as givens rather than a choice that should be subjected to constant review, reappraisal, and renegotiation.

As this discussion suggests, there are really two kinds of policy. One kind is imbedded in the routines of organizations and in the technology they use. The other kind of policy is found in plans, regulations, mission statements, legislative mandates, and the like. The first kind of policy is intrinsic and imbedded, the second kind explicit and overt. Imbedded policies are more basic, less visible and more difficult to renegotiate and change. It is the imbedded policies of the transit industry that have changed little over the last five decades—a period of dramatic change in the spatial structure and temporal rhythms of American cities.

Because it has changed so little, the transit industry has become *structurally obsolete*: its form suits the functions and markets that transit served at the turn of the century; it no longer matches up very well with the functions and markets that transit serves today. Indeed, structural obsolescence goes a long way toward explaining transit's impaired earning power and its persistent financial distress.

As you may judge from the paragraph above, this book is an argumentative one. Its goal is to provoke a constructive debate about the kind of transit services that would be appropriate for the modern American city. To achieve this goal, it tells the story of transit's growth and decline and assesses the performance of recent policies and programs designed to preserve and revitalize transit service. It concludes that subsidy has not stabilized the industry and that compound changes in transit's basic way of doing business are necessary if mass transit is to play a significant role in the future of urban transportation.

The book was written because I found that many of my students in transportation engineering and city planning knew little about the history of American cities, or their transit systems. The biggest gap in their understanding was a knowledge of the market conditions which prevailed in the era when transit was the dominant means of city transportation. Most students were surprised to learn, for example, that Sunday was once the day of heaviest transit patronage, that the profitability of many streetcar systems hinged on doing a booming business during the holiday season, and that many transit systems were vendors of electricity and real estate, as well as transportation. These facts are more than historical trivia. They go a long way toward explaining why transit was once profitable and requires subsidy today.

My students also started with a hazy idea of the dynamics of transit's decline. Many thought that transit's decline began in the late 1940s, and therefore concluded that it coincided with the construction of urban freeways and the explosive growth of metropolitan suburbs. They were surprised to learn that transit systems had lost investor confidence by the first decade of this century, that disinvestment began as early as 1916, and that business failures occurred frequently in the 1920s.

It goes without saying that accurate diagnosis is necessary for effective prescription. This is why it is essential to understand history before setting out to make or revise policy. Had the transit policies of the 1960s and 1970s been informed by a better understanding of history, they might have proved considerably more effective. For example, more attention might have been paid to the need for industrial reorganization as opposed to giving first priority to the replacement of aging equipment and the extension and expansion of service. But, history was ignored, and the conversion of transit from public to private ownership was foregone as an opportunity to reorganize the industry and modernize it in more than cosmetic ways.

Public ownership *has* provided a reprieve for transit, but it has not restored the industry to a stable footing. Indeed, more and more subsidy has been required each succeeding year to keep systems operating and passengers riding.

Subsidy for transit is necessary and appropriate, but endlessly increasing subsidy is both inappropriate and unrealistic. It is time, in short, to consider the reorganization alternative—as difficult and painful as it may be. One strategy of reorganization and renewal is sketched out in the final chapter. The steps proposed are controversial—as I suspect this book may be. Controversy is not its objective. Its goal is to prompt constructive discussion and debate about how to change the form of transit so that it fits the modern American city.

A draft of this manuscript served this purpose well in my graduate course on Transportation Policy. I hope it will prove equally useful for courses that deal with transit planning, urban transportation planning, transportation economics, urban history, and urban policy.

DAVID W. JONES, JR.

1

MASS TRANSIT—A DISTRESSED INDUSTRY AND AN ESSENTIAL PUBLIC SERVICE

INTRODUCTION

"Mass transit" is a shorthand term used to describe a family of public transportation services that traces its lineage to the street railways that dominated city transportation in the first decade of the twentieth century. Mass transit service is provided by streetcar, subway, and rapid transit, by motorbus, and by trolleybus. Electric streetcars, subways, and rapid transit systems were introduced in the 1890s; the diffusion of buses and trolleybuses occurred later—in the 1920s. As did the street railways that preceded them, most transit operations offer services on fixed routes against a fixed schedule for a flat fare.

Transit services are typically organized on a monopoly basis with a single carrier providing service over a relatively large urban territory. This organizational format, like many of the industry's other operating customs, dates to the street railway era.

Knowing about the history and lineage of mass transit is absolutely essential for understanding the modern industry and the way in which it does business. Tradition, custom, and historical obligation explain many of transit's current service features, fare policies, and operating customs. If we could reinvent transit, figuratively starting from scratch, we most probably would invent an industry with very different work rules, a different fare structure, and a different approach to service delivery. It would provide a wider diversity of services, use labor in more diverse ways, and provide its workers with a wider range of promotion opportunities. But transit cannot be reinvented from scratch; it must be renewed and reorganized from within.

Renewal is important because mass transit is an essential public service—but one that is increasingly costly to sustain. The service that transit provides is essential because the downtown business districts of many of the nation's largest cities depend on it for their access to labor and customers. Transit is also essential because it plays an important role in the lives of many of those who are unable to drive or afford automobile ownership. But preserving the industry so that it can perform these important roles has required massive and steadily increasing subsidy.[1] Preserving service is costly because transit has a grave productivity problem and because its way of doing business is, in many ways, obsolete. The way in which transit service is organized matches the travel patterns of the early twentieth century; it does not fit transit's current role in the scheme of urban transportation—a role that is supplemental and subordinate to that of the automobile.

This book amounts to a search for a strategy of reorganization and renewal for mass transit. The search is necessary because mass transit is both an essential service and a competitive failure. More precisely, mass transit is a social service operated in the manner of a public enterprise by organizations that have passed from private to public ownership through a gradual process of economic attrition and competitive failure. Public ownership and public subsidy have not restored the industry to a stable competitive footing. Even with subsidy, the industry continues to experience recurrent financial crises that jeopardize its reliability as a public service.

Before we can conceive and propose a way in which to preserve and reorganize transit service, we must understand the industry, its markets, and the policy environment in which it operates. We must also persuade the reader that reorganization is both necessary and desirable.

THE INDUSTRY

Mass transit is part of the larger public transportation industry that includes

Buses or streetcars operated on surface streets subject to cross traffic

Subway, elevated, and rail rapid transit services operated on exclusive rights-of-way

Commuter railroad services operated on trackage often shared with freight traffic

Taxis and other paratransit operations called or hailed into service on demand rather than on schedule

Each kind of public transportation has a unique history, unique business traditions, and a unique set of labor-management relations. Each operation is also idiosyncratic, a creature of local market conditions and local institutional arrangements. Their generic link is a commonality of legal standing. All are obligated to provide service to any and all willing customers at posted rates, and all are obliged to exercise a strenuous standard of care for passenger safety. Another common link is a history of financial distress and, until recently, a history of declining service and patronage.

Our analysis will focus on mass transit—the workhorses of the public transportation industry. We will discuss the financial problems of railroad commutation, but emphasis will be given to the problems and prospects of properties that provide bus, subway, or rapid transit service.

THE MARKET FOR TRANSIT

Mass transit can be characterized as an urban or big-city phenomenon because most transit trip making occurs in cities with populations that exceed 1 million. In 1970, for example, 70 percent of all mass transit trips were made in the nation's 15 largest metropolitan areas.[2] In these centers and elsewhere, the majority of transit trips are those made by workers traveling to and from jobs located in downtown business districts. Table 1-1 shows the percentage of work-trip travel served by public transportation (mass transit, taxicab, and commuter railroad) in 18 of the nation's largest metropolitan areas. It shows that public transportation plays a much more important role in central cities than it does in metropolitan suburbs and that metropolitan areas are developing in a fashion that is less and less reliant on mass transit.

Although city size is an important correlate of the demand for transit service, the heaviest transit use occurs in a special class of cities distinguished by their age as well as their size. Seventy-five percent of all transit travel is concentrated in older cities that reached the population plateau of 100,000 by 1890 and 250,000 by 1920.[3] These were the nation's dominant manufacturing and finance centers during the early years of the industrial era. Today, these older American cities account for less than 25 percent of the nation's urban population, and almost all have lost resident population since the 1950s. The decline of their resident population is one of many reasons for transit's financial distress.

TABLE 1-1 Percentage of the Work Force Using Transit
for the Journey to Work in 18 Metropolitan Areas

City	Percentage of Central City Workers Using Transit in 1970	Percentage of the Metropolitan Work Force Using Transit in 1970	1980
New York	56	43	36
Boston	36	18	16
Newark	32	14	11
San Francisco	32	15	17
Philadelphia	32	17	14
Chicago	30	19	18
Pittsburgh	29	14	12
New Orleans	26	20	11
Washington	25	16	16
Baltimore	21	13	11
Cleveland	20	13	13
Buffalo	18	10	7
Milwaukee	17	12	7
Detroit	15	8	4
St. Louis	13	8	6
Cincinnati	12	8	7
Miami	12	9	6
Seattle	11	7	10

Source: U.S. Census Bureau, The Journey to Work (Washington, D.C.: Government Printing Office, 1980).

Another characteristic of the residual market for transit service is its extreme temporal imbalance. The imbalance of transit traffic—heavy use during the rush hours and sharply lower patronage during the mid-day and on weekends—contributes significantly to the industry's impaired earning power. Scaling the capacity of systems to serve the peak imposes a significant financial burden on transit properties because much of the labor and equipment necessary for the rush hour cannot be used productively during the rest of the day.

More than any other factor, peaking explains why public transportation must be subsidized if it is to play a significant role in serving the commuter. Transit, of course, did not always require subsidy, and so it is instructive to compare the time profile of transit use today with that prevailing in the first decade of the century when transit was last considered an attractive private investment. Table 1-2 compares the time pattern of usage for two roughly comparable transit systems, the Boston Elevated in 1915 and Bay Area (San Francisco) Rapid Transit in 1980.

In snowy climates, the daily rhythms of the peak are amplified by

TABLE 1-2 The Changing Time Pattern of Transit Usage

	Boston Elevated, 1915	BART, 1980
Weekday patronage as a percentage of weekly	73%	88%
Saturday as a percentage of weekly	17	8
Sundays as a percentage of weekly	10	4
Morning and evening peaks as a percentage of daily	39	48

Sources: Edward S. Mason, *The Street Railway in Massachusetts* (Cambridge, Mass.: Harvard University Press, 1932) and Metropolitan Transportation Commission, *Traffic Survey Series—Bay Bridge* (Berkeley, Calif.: MTC, 1980).

seasonal ridership fluctuations that impose greater demands on transit systems during the winter than during the fair-weather months. Providing safe and reliable transportation in blizzard conditions is another way that mass transit functions as an essential social service.[4] In this role, transit is somewhat analogous to fire protection; it performs a function whose value should be measured as much by the readiness to serve as by the service actually rendered.

THE INDUSTRY'S POLICY ENVIRONMENT

Until the late 1950s, most urban mass transportation services were operated by private companies organized on a for-profit basis. While organized as profit-making enterprises, the urban transit properties that are the workhorses of the industry have been financially troubled since World War I.[5] During the depression and in the years following World War II, the industry's financial distress became acute, and the largest urban properties were reorganized as public enterprises. Public ownership did not stabilize the revenues or ridership of most properties, and the trend of industrywide decline continued.[6] The waves of fare increases and service reduction that occurred during the 1950s prompted an extended debate over the obligation of the federal government to subsidize the industry.

Congress took up the subsidy debate in 1960, authorizing a program of low-interest loans the following year. Federal involvement was expanded with the authorization of grants for capital investments such as the purchase of rolling stock, the construction of facilities, and the acquisition of properties still in private ownership. The capital subsidy program was approved in 1964 and expanded significantly in 1972. Finally, in 1974, Congress approved operating subsidies—direct payments to offset operating expenses. By 1978, federal subsidies could be used for virtually any public transportation purpose proposed by local governments. These included

The purchase of both new and replacement equipment

The purchase of right-of-way and the construction of terminals

The payment of operating as well as capital expenses

The introduction of new suburban services as well as the acquisition of older urban properties still in private ownership

The operation of services in rural townships as well as metropolitan centers

The purchase of service from railroads or taxi companies as well as direct payments to public transit agencies

Table 1-3 shows the step-by-step progression of deepening federal involvement in transit finance.

Critics of transit subsidies have noted that Congress "backed into" a deeper and deeper commitment to mass transit without reaching agreement on the objectives to be achieved and without anticipating the eventual cost of federal involvement.[7] Such criticism is valid. Congress mapped transit policy and authorized eventually massive expenditures without careful appraisal of the reasons transit was in financial distress or a clear understanding of what subsidy would accomplish. Federal subsidies were approved without systematic inquiry into the ability of local government to shoulder the cost of subsidy without federal assistance. And federal aid was made universally available without reference to any standard of need or measure of merit.

The expansion of the transit aid program was propelled by the growing electoral and political influence of urban constituencies in the 1960s and 1970s.[8] The result was a program that was sensitive to the concerns of urban and suburban constituencies, balanced geographically to ensure broad-based congressional support but handicapped by the lack of a clear mandate or defined objectives.[9] Erected on a foundation of political commitments rather than clear national purposes, the program was vulnerable to a change in political ideology or presidential philosophy. The presidential election of 1980 marked such a change, and the expansionist trend of federal involvement in mass transit was reversed abruptly by the Reagan administration. Thus, the 1980 presidential election was a turning point for federal involvement in mass transit as well as other domestic spending programs. The Reagan administration proposed the elimination of federal subsidies for

TABLE 1-3 Landmark Congressional Actions in the Evolution
of Federal Assistance for Mass Transit, 1961-1978

Year	Congressional Actions
1961	Authorized loans and demonstration grants for the providers of urban mass transportation services.
1964	Appropriated general revenues for a program of capital grants to build or replace transit facilities, purchase transit coaches, and acquire private transit properties. Established a federal-local matching ratio of 67 to 33 and imposed a 12.5 percent ceiling on each state's share of the program total.
1970	Augmented spending authority significantly, allowing multiyear commitments for capital-intensive projects such as rapid transit facilities. Eliminated the 12.5 percent per state limit on program shares.
1973	Increased federal matching rate from 67 to 80 percent. Authorized use of highway user revenues for selected transit purposes.
1974	Authorized transit operating subsidies for urbanized areas. Established 50:50 matching ratio for operating assistance, requiring localities to sustain local tax support as a condition of operating assistance.
1978	Extended transit operating subsidies to small cities. Relaxed requirement for sustained local tax support. Augmented operating assistance for cities with rail transit systems.

transit operations and reduced the growth of the capital grant program as well.

Although it seems unlikely that Congress will acquiesce to the complete withdrawal of operating subsidies, the Reagan proposals signal the end of an era and auger a reduction in federal aid. Thus, it is an appropriate time to assess what was accomplished during two decades of active federal involvement in urban transit finance. Our analysis will be based on two constellations of data. One is the performance record of the transit industry in the period of federal subsidy. The other is the historical record of transit's development and subsequent decline—its performance in the period 1890 to 1960.

THE DYNAMICS OF TRANSIT'S FINANCIAL DISTRESS

As we shall see, federal transit policy was built on a fundamental misapprehension of the dynamics of transit's financial distress. That distress has two dimensions. The first is impaired earning power—an inability to price services in relation to their cost without significant loss of ridership. The second is cost escalation—a rate of cost increase out of proportion with its rate of revenue growth.

The root causes of transit's impaired earning power are structural:

1. Most service is provided at a flat fare incompatible with a pattern of traffic that peaks during morning and evening rush hours.
2. The industry has been expected to provide universal service despite the incompatibility of its cost structure with the provision of nighttime service or local service in low-density suburbs.
3. The industry has limited pricing discretion and particularly limited ability to adjust fares upward in small increments so as to offset increasing costs—a significant liability in periods of rapid inflation.

The root causes of cost increases in excess of inflation are also structural:

1. The industry's monopoly format has enhanced the bargaining power of transit labor, making cost discipline difficult and contributing to the outsized growth of operating expenses.
2. The industry's service mix and promotion policies are such that transit workers are unable to better their standard of living by advancing to positions of increasing responsibility and productivity; the base wage must be steadily increased if workers are to improve their standard of living.
3. Work rules have been negotiated on the basis of parity with manufacturing workers despite a trade pattern more closely analogous to that of merchandizing operations that employ part-time labor to serve periods of peak demand.

The federal policy of the 1960s and 1970s responded to the first of transit's problems—its impaired earning power—through subsidy. It did not address the exponentiation of operating costs and, thus, was unable to restore the industry to a stable footing.

The program that Congress created in the 1960s and 1970s was based on the widely held, but historically invalid, view that transit's decline was caused by the "imbalance" of public spending for highways and public transportation, by the failure to plan for orderly urban development, and by the "downward spiral" of ridership caused by fare increases and service reductions.

Congress embraced this theory of transit's decline, attributing the industry's economic distress to failings of public policy: spending for highways that placed transit at unfair competitive disadvantage relative to the private automobile and laissez-faire attitudes toward land use that permitted sprawling and scattered urban development.

The transit aid program that was constructed in the 1960s and 1970s was based on this theory of transit's decline.[10] It sought to "balance" federal spending for transit and highways, encourage regional planning and metropolitan growth management, and stabilize transit fares through operating subsidies. Thus, federal policy was erected on the assumption that public transportation could be placed on a stable competitive footing without significant changes in its fare structure, its cost structure, its service philosophy, or its labor relations.

Our analysis shows that subsidies have *not* stabilized the transit industry. A stable transit industry would not "turn a profit" in the conventional business sense, but it *would* maintain a stable balance between the growth rates of costs and revenues, and ridership and productivity, thus avoiding recurrent financial crisis. By this standard, stabilization has not been achieved. Productivity has continued to decline, and unit costs continue to increase. Between 1972 and 1980, the period of ridership recovery, transit subsidy increased 265 percent in real dollar terms while ridership increased by only 25 percent.[11] These are alarmingly disparate rates of change.

The trend of transit operating costs is also disturbing: cost per passenger increased 87 percent from 1960 to 1972 and another 10 percent from 1972 to 1980.[12] Thus, the trend of both costs and operating deficits belies any contention that subsidy has restored transit to a stable financial footing. Indeed, the performance of the transit industry during the period of federal involvement reveals its continuing financial distress; this, in turn, poses a set of interesting and difficult questions:

Is there a course of action that *would* stabilize the industry?

What form would it take?

Is it feasible to implement?

To begin to answer these questions, we must understand the underlying causes of transit's continuing economic distress. As we shall see, transit's financial problems are deeply rooted in the industry's developmental history and in the inadequacy of its response to social change.

A PREVIEW OF TRANSIT'S DEVELOPMENTAL HISTORY

The nation's large urban transit properties—their fare structure, their cost structure, their operating philosophy, and their labor relations—are artifacts of the horsecar and streetcar eras. A pattern of pricing, service delivery, and labor relations erected before the turn of the century has survived to the present with remarkably little change.[13] Transit properties have been transformed from for-profit enterprises in private ownership to subsidized agencies in public ownership, and the industry's dominant technology has changed from the horsecar to the electric trolley to the diesel motorbus, but these changes are relatively superficial. In other, more basic ways the industry has changed little since the 1890s, the period of electrification and consolidation of street railways. But its environment has changed profoundly since the first decade of the twentieth century—the last decade of economic stability for public transportation. In the first decade of the twentieth century, six-day workweeks were the norm; transit attracted large numbers of off-peak recreation and excursion travelers; it served compact cities in which crowding, not sprawl, was the nemesis of social reformers; it employed a labor force whose wages were depressed by an historically unparalleled level of migration; and its primary competition was afforded by merchants of shoe leather. As important, inflation was mild and was offset by intermittent cycles of deflation.

Due in part to restrictive regulatory policies and its obligations as a monopoly, transit was unable to adapt to the social change that resulted from the growth of urban wealth, the nearly universal diffusion of the automobile, and the patterns of urban growth that accompanied increasing incomes and increasing automobile ownership. These forces of social change began to remake cities in the 1920s. Indeed, the decade of the 1920s marked the beginning of the decline in transit ridership and revenues.

But transit was a financially troubled industry even before the 1920s. Transit's impaired earning power was already evident to investors by 1908, and, as a consequence, few transit properties were able to finance the service improvements needed to compete favorably with the automobile in the 1920s.[14] Transit was, in short, a financially troubled industry *before* the advent of automotive competition and long before the era of massive public investment in urban freeways. Considering the duration of transit's financial distress, it whould not be surprising that the federal aid program of the 1960s and 1970s was insufficient to restore transit to a stable competitive footing.

Stabilizing the industry will require structural change—change in its basic way of doing business and change in the pattern of labor relations that has characterized the industry since World War I. The changes required are thoroughgoing and fundamental, and it is our view that they cannot be implemented without the active and constructive involvement of the federal government.

What changes in the organization and operation of transit services are needed? And can those changes be accomplished? These are central questions, but we plan to defer their discussion for the moment. Before answering them, we propose to lead readers along the step-by-step path of analysis, reasoning—and worry—that we traveled to reach the conclusions and recommendations presented in the last chapter of the book. Our conclusions are the product of inquiry into the performance of federal transit policy and analysis of the causes of transit's long-standing financial distress. By the time we reach the closing chapters, we hope that you will share our concern and our conclusion: that transit services are too important to forfeit through attrition—but too costly to perpetuate without change.

NOTES

1. Institute of Public Administration, *Financing Transit: Alternatives for Local Government* (Washington, D.C.: U.S. Department of Transportation, 1979), pp. 8-19.

2. Arthur Saltzman and Richard J. Solomon, "Historical Overview of the Decline of the Transit Industry," *Highway Research Record*, No. 417 (1972), p. 9.

3. Twenty cities fall in this class. Their 1975 share of all transit trip making was estimated from data reported in American Public Transit Association, *Transit Operating Report, 1975* (Washington, D.C.: APTA, 1976).

4. As this discussion indicates, transit is not an essential public service in any absolute or intrinsic sense. Unlike public education or police protection, there is no universal need for public transportation. It is essential only in those situations where the functions it performs could not be replaced without extreme disruption or excessive cost. Its essentiality is fungible, not absolute.

5. Edward S. Mason, *The Street Railway in Massachusetts* (Cambridge, Mass.: Harvard University Press, 1932), pp. 7-17; Emerson P. Schmidt, *Industrial Relations in Urban Transportation* (Minneapolis: University of Minnesota Press, 1937), pp. 41-47.

6. Until the 1960s, most publicly owned transit properties were organized as public authorities—enterprises expected to pay their expense of operation and debt service but not dividends.

7. Senator Harrison Williams, sponsor of the first transit aid legislation, described federal involvement as "the breakthrough that will lead to major efforts at self-recovery by the local public and private institutions, enabling them to go the rest of the way alone." See Subcommittee on Housing, Senate Committee on Banking and Currency, *Hearings on S. 345* (Washington, D.C.: Government Printing Office, 1961), p. 36.

8. Michael N. Danielson, *Federal-Metropolitan Politics and the Commuter Crisis* (New York: Columbia University Press, 1965), p. 174.

9. George M. Smerk, *Urban Mass Transportation: A Dozen Years of Federal Policy* (Bloomington: Indiana University Press, 1974), pp. 250-256.

10. The diagnostic content of early federal transit policy may be inferred from key testimony to be found in the 1961 and 1962 hearing records. See especially the statements of Senator Harrison Williams; Mayor Richardson Dilworth, president, U.S. Conference of Mayors; Luther Gulick, president, Institute of Public

Administration; and William L. C. Wheaton, chairman, Policy Committee, National Housing Conference, in *Hearings on S. 345,* Senate Banking Committee, 1961. See also the "Joint Report to the President by the Secretary of Commerce and the Housing and Home Finance Administrator," in *Hearings on H.R. 11158,* House Banking and Currency Committee (Washington, D.C.: Government Printing Office, 1962), pp. 36-50.

11. Estimated from data reported in American Public Transit Association, *Transit Fact Book, 1981* (Washington, D.C.: APTA, 1981), p. 52; see also pp. 46-47.

12. Ibid.

13. Schmidt, *Industrial Relations in Urban Transportation,* pp. 71-101.

14. John I. Beggs, "Address of the President," 1907 Convention of the American Street and Interurban Railway Association (New York: ASIRA, 1907), pp. 63-64. See, also, The American Electric Railway Association, *The Urban Transportation Problem* (New York: AERA, circa 1933), pp. 15-16.

2

TRANSIT INDUSTRY PERFORMANCE:
1902 TO 1982

INTRODUCTION

The transit policies that Congress shaped in the 1960s and 1970s were based on the premise that the decline of public transportation is a postwar phenomenon. On first inspection, this premise appears reasonable because aggregate nationwide ridership did not peak until 1946 and precipitous decline did not begin until the postwar period. As Figure 2-1 shows, transit patronage increased from 1900 through the mid-1920s, leveled off and declined fractionally after middecade, then plunged downward during the first years of the Great Depression. Patronage staged a modest recovery in the mid-1930s and then rebounded dramatically during World War II. Precipitous decline began in the late 1940s and continued through the 1950s. More gradual decline characterized the trend of ridership in the 1960s and early 1970s. Ridership recovered in the mid-1970s, but faltered again after 1980.

Examining Figure 2-1, it might seem appropriate to conclude that transit was a casualty of the postwar milieu: the return of prosperity, the growth of the suburbs, the construction of urban freeways, and the exodus of the middle class from central cities. Interpreting these contemporaneous events, economists have stressed that the automobile is used in complementarity with single-family housing and that suburbanization stimulates auto use and results in its substitution for travel by transit.[1] Many planners have used stronger language to describe the same concurrence of events; they argue that transit was the victim of

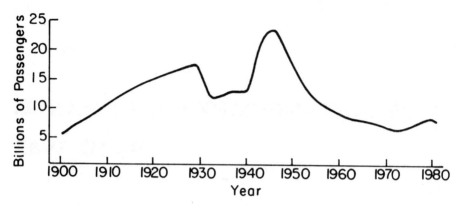

Source: American Public Transit Association, *Transit Fact Book, 1981*, Washington, D.C.: APTA, 1981.

Figure 2-1 The Major Trends of Transit Ridership—1900–1980

laissez-faire land-use policies, sprawl development, and public spending for highway construction and home mortgage assistance—all of which combined to stimulate suburban growth.

The "casualty" or "victim" theory of transit's decline is the diagnostic foundation on which federal transit policy was built. Transit lost competitive advantage, the theory posits, because postwar freeway, land-use, and housing policies fostered a pattern of urban settlement that is incompatible with efficient transit operation.[2] The result has been characterized as a self-fulfilling prophesy or a self-sustaining growth dynamic: freeway construction made automobile ownership and suburban location more attractive; in turn, increased travel by car generated additional gas tax revenues to pay for more freeway construction, further enhancing the attractiveness of suburban location and fueling the growth spiral of suburbs, freeways, and auto use.

As the ownership and use of automobiles increased, transit was buffeted by a countervailing downward spiral: diversion of patronage to the automobile forced service reductions that further eroded patronage and revenues, necessitating fare increases and accelerating the loss of ridership.

As many planners have interpreted these events, unbalanced public policy is the causal nexus of transit's decline. Transit declined because government failed to counterbalance the effect of public spending for highways and mortgage assistance with land-use controls and financial aid for mass transit. Thus, diagnosis merged with prescription, creating a philosophical imperative for transit subsidy and metropolitan growth management.[3] Such were the intellectual foundations of federal transit policy during the 1960s and 1970s and the origins of the prescriptive commitment to "balanced transportation," "balanced growth," and "rational urban form."

REINTERPRETING THE TREND OF PATRONAGE

First inspection recommends the casualty theory of transit's decline, but closer examination will show that postwar suburbanization only compounded the distress of an already troubled and declining industry. As we shall see, the demand for conventional transit service actually began to decline at middecade in the 1920s, and the transit industry's financial distress can be dated to the period before World War I.

Before we can expect the reader to accept this statement, we must reconcile an apparent contradiction: the *fact* that transit patronage peaked in 1946 and our *assertion* that the demand for conventional transit service actually began to decline in the 1920s. This requires a closer examination of Figure 2-1, which offers a faithful accounting of the trend of transit patronage, but also a misleading one. It is misleading because the volatile movements of the patronage trendline that occurred during the depression, World War II and the postwar normalization period were fundamentally anomalous. The collapse of patronage during the 1930s reflects the stringencies of depression whereas the emphatic recovery of the period 1942–1946 reflects the exigencies of war: gas and tire rationing, voluntary conservation, the suspension of automobile production, spot shortages of gasoline and auto parts, billeted travel by servicemen, and outsized employment levels attributable to war production. Thus, the recovery of patronage during World War II and its 1946 highwater mark are not the product of a healthy industry operating at peak performance. Rather, the 1942–1946 patronage crest is an artifact of wartime necessity, hardship, and sacrifice. It significantly overstates the demand for transit that would have prevailed under conditions of stable peacetime employment.

Estimates prepared by the American Transit Association during World War II are helpful in assessing the extent to which the wartime peak in ridership should be attributed to emergency conditions.[4] Figure 2-2 shows the ATA's estimate of the ridership induced by gas and tire rationing and the suspension of automobile production. Wartime ridership was also inflated by the travel of servicemen away from home and by the work trips of the so-called "provisionally employed"—women and teenagers who entered the labor force for the duration of the wartime emergency with the result that total employment greatly exceeded "normal" peacetime levels.[5] Our approximation of the ridership attributable to travel by servicemen and "excess employment" is also shown

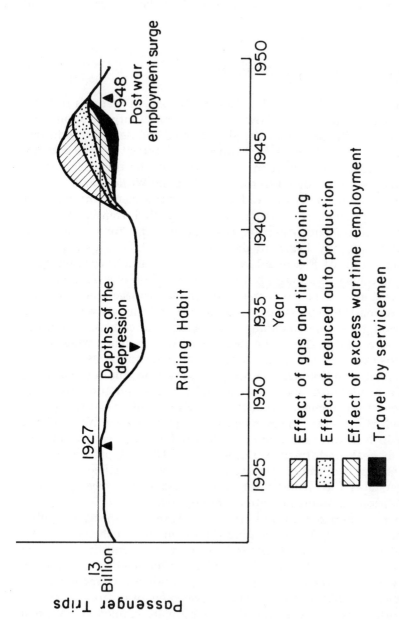

Source: Charles Stephenson, "Transit's Prospects for Postwar Traffic" (Washington, D.C.: American Transit Association, 1944) and supplemental calculations by the author based on wartime and postwar employment statistics.

Figure 2-2 Decomposition of the 1941–1946 Ridership Peak

in Figure 2-2. It establishes that the 1942–1946 patronage peak cannot be attributed to the play of choice and habit, cost, and service quality that would normally size transit's share of the travel market during periods of stable peacetime employment. It also shows that wartime economic recovery restored discretionary ridership, but only to a level approximating that recorded during the last full-employment years of the 1920s. In turn, this argues that the precipitous decline in transit ridership that followed World War II was, in large measure, a return to normalcy—a predictable shakeout attributable to postwar normalization and the economics of demobilization.

This is not a novel assertion. The American Transit Association interpreted 1946 ridership as an historical aberration in formal testimony before Congress in 1961.[6] Testifying in favor of transit subsidies, the executive vice president of the ATA said,

> In their appearances before regulatory bodies during the postwar period, a great many transit companies have used 1946 as the base for measuring the extent of the decline in riding which they have experienced. *We all know that 1946 was an artificial peak.* A number of transit companies were hauling at that time three or four times as many people as they handled prewar.

> But by using the 1946 base they are able to show a more drastic decline in riding than would otherwise be the case if you used, for example, 1940 as the base. They have done this to try to impress the regulatory people with the need for granting fare increases. . . . When we came out of this war period we knew that this riding was going to decline. . . . We were at an artificial peak by virtue of the rationing that was in effect, (and) the fact that no automobiles had been produced. People were literally riding on the roof as far as some transit companies were concerned.

Clearly, then, ridership counts from the depression years significantly understate "normal" discretionary demand for transit service, and counts from World War II and the extended normalization period that followed it significantly overstate discretionary demand. Ridership statistics for this entire 20-year period are anomalous and, in that sense, artificial. They mask rather than reveal the transit industry's real market potential.

If the patronage statistics for the 1930s and 1940s are anomalous and artificial, what yardstick should we use to gauge the true trend of demand for transit service? Or, stated another way, What would the secular trend of transit ridership have looked like in the absence of depression and war? The answer to this question will help us to understand the extent to which transit was a healthy industry that fell victim to postwar housing, land-use, and freeway development policies.

We can begin by examining the trend of ridership in the 1920s—an epoch that warrants detailed understanding because it was a period of relative normalcy in which ridership and discretionary demand can be equated. It also deserves serious study because middecade marks the high-water mark of transit ridership if one accepts the proposition that the patronage of the mid-1940s was a wartime anomaly.

PATRONAGE IN THE 1920s

Table 2-1 shows the aggregate nationwide trend of transit ridership during the full-employment years of the 1920s. These estimates, made by the ATA and its successor, the American Public Transit Association, show that ridership peaked in either 1926 or 1927—either three or four years prior to the depression. The loss of ridership shown in Table 2-1 is hardly a large one. Without corroborative evidence, it could be dismissed as accounting error, incomplete reporting, or a cyclic fluctuation in the patronage level. Segmenting ridership statistics by city size, type of operation, size of operation, type of market, and geographic region offers a way to assess whether such a small change signals the true beginnings of transit's secular decline.

    Table 2-2 shows seven ways of classifying transit markets and the results of the segmentation analysis. Its message is that ridership growth

TABLE 2-1 Transit Ridership, 1921–1929
(billions of passenger trips)

Year	ATA[1]	APTA[2]
1921	15.2	14.6
1922	16.2	15.7
1923	16.7	16.3
1924	16.6	16.3
1925	16.7	16.7
1926	17.1	17.2
1927	16.9	17.3
1928	16.5	17.0
1929	16.4	17.0
Percentage loss of ridership from peak year to 1929	−4.3%	−1.7%

[1] American Transit Association, *Transit Journal*, January 1936.

[2] See American Public Transport Association estimates as reported in *Moody's Transportation Manual.* (New York: Moody's Investors Service, Inc., 1981.)

TABLE 2-2 Transit Patronage in the 1920s: A Disaggregate Analysis

Method of Disaggregation	Patronage Trend by Submarket
By city size	Ridership growth was confined to cities with populations in excess of 1 million. Ridership decline is evident in cities of every other size class.[1]
By type of operation	Ridership of bus lines and rapid transit systems was increasing while streetcar ridership was declining. The growth of bus and rapid transit ridership was insufficient to offset the decline of streetcar patronage.[2]
By type of service	Properties operating excursion services experienced more severe erosion of ridership than did properties operating urban services only, but decline was the norm for both groups.[3]
By locus of service	Urban ridership slumped into decline *before* suburban ridership; both declined after 1927. This seeming anomaly is explained by the growth of suburban bus service that occurred as transit properties expanded their territories to compete with the automobile.[4]
By geographic region	Streetcar ridership declined in every region of the country with the exception of the Middle Atlantic Region anchored by New York City and the Gulf States Region anchored by New Orleans.[5]
By state	Growth in streetcar ridership was confined to the states of New York, Pennsylvania, Illinois, California, Kentucky, and Alabama.[6]
By time of day and day of the week	Commuter ridership during weekday rush hours was increasing, but these gains were offset by steady erosion of patronage on Sundays, holidays, and during the off peak.[7]

[1] See American Transit Association, *The Urban Transportation Problem* (New York: ATA, circa 1933).

[2] See *ibid*. and American Transit Association, *Transit Journal*, January 1936.

[3] See American Electric Railway Association, *Electric Railway Operations in 1925* Bulletin No. 77 (1926).

[4] See American Transit Association, *Transit Fact Book Supplement*, December 1966.

[5] See U.S. Bureau of the Census, *Electric Railways and Affiliated Motor Bus Lines* (Washington, D.C.: Government Printing Office, 1931).

[6] See *ibid*.

[7] See Emerson P. Schmidt, *Industrial Relations in Urban Transportation* (Minneapolis: University of Minnesota Press, 1937); Edward S. Mason, *The Street Railway in Massachusetts* (Cambridge, Mass.: Harvard University Press, 1932).

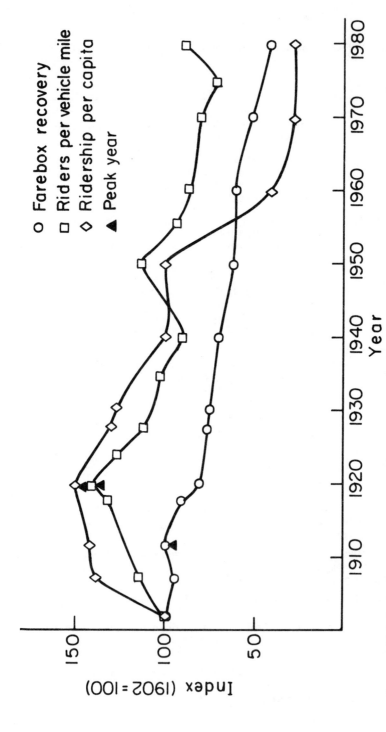

Figure 2-3 Transit Performance: 1902–1980

Sources: U.S. Bureau of the Census, *Electric Railways and Affiliated Motor Bus Lines* (Washington, D.C.: U.S. Government Printing Office, 1931); U.S. Bureau of the Census, *Historical Statistics of the United States* (Washington, D.C.: U.S. Government Printing Office, 1976); *Moody's Transportation Manual* (New York: Moody's Investors Services, Inc., 1981); American Public Transit Association, *Transit Fact Book* (Washington, D.C.: APTA, 1976 and 1981).

was still occurring in some markets, but at a rate insufficient to offset the substitution of travel by auto for travel by transit in other markets. Ridership growth was occurring in the largest cities, and rush-hour ridership seems to have been growing in many cities, both large and small. But midday, excursion, and weekend ridership was declining steadily as was total ridership in cities with a population less than 1 million. As a consequence, the trend of ridership in the aggregate was net negative.

The pattern of mixed performance evident from our disaggregate analysis is precisely what one would expect of an industry losing momentum and then slumping over the crest of its growth curve into secular decline. It provides corroborative evidence that the true peak of the transit industry's market performance occurred in the mid-1920s.

Further corroboration is provided by performance indicators other than ridership. Figure 2-3 shows the trend of three such indicators: ridership per capita, a measure of transit's share of the travel market; ridership per vehicle mile, a measure of operational productivity; and farebox recovery, a measure of the industry's earning power. Table 2-3 shows the trend of net capital expenditures, a measure of investor confidence and the industry's standing in the capital markets. From these exhibits it is evident that transit's earning power has declined steadily

TABLE 2-3 Net Capital Expenditures
of Urban Transit Properties, 1890–1950

Year	Net Expenditures (in millions of 1929 dollars)
1890	$ 74.0
1895	176.2
1900	170.9
1905	229.8
1910	66.1
1915	15.2
1920	−128.5 [a]
1925	−105.4 [a]
1930	−85.3 [a]
1935	−60.7 [a]
1940	−10.4 [a]
1945	−58.4 [a]
1950	−53.5 [a]

[a] Negative expenditure, that is, disinvestment.

Source: M. J. Ulmer, Capital in Transportation, Communications, and Public Utilities (Princeton, N.J.: Princeton University Press, 1960), Tables F-1 and G-1.

since 1912, that investment peaked in 1905, and that the peaks of both productivity and market penetration were reached in 1922.

Finally, Table 2-4 shows that traffic density—passenger miles per vehicle mile—also peaked in 1922. The same table shows the only two measures of transit industry output that were trending upward in the 1920s: vehicle miles of service rendered and passenger miles of service consumed. The increase in vehicle miles and passenger miles is attributable to suburban service extensions. Increasing the reach of service proved effective in generating peak-hour ridership among suburban commuters, hence, the growth trend of passenger mileage, but it did not stabilize overall ridership or the industry's financial position.[7] Gains in the peak were offset by the steady erosion of off-peak and weekend travel. The erosion of transit's off-peak ridership began in this period as shown in Table 2-5. It shows that gross patronage counts mask a very significant change in the composition of transit's patronage base that was occurring in the 1920s. This shift in the composition of transit traffic is attributable to the increasing use of automobiles for excursion travel, shopping trips, and travel as a family group. From the 1920s onward, the social and recreational life of American communities would be fashioned around the automobile, leaving transit with the obligation but not the financial wherewithal to serve travel to work. Table 2-5 shows that peak-hour ridership actually *increased* during the 1920s as properties extended service to the suburbs in the effort to

TABLE 2-4 Coach and Passenger Miles of Service, 1921–1929
(in billions)

Year	Vehicle Miles[1]	Passenger Miles[2]	Passenger Miles per Vehicle Mile[3]
1921	2.12	55.8	6.9
1922	2.16	60.6	7.3
1923	2.28	63.6	7.2
1924	2.43	65.2	6.7
1925	2.58	68.3	6.5
1926	2.78	71.8	6.2
1927	2.92	73.3	5.9
1928	3.00	73.6	5.7
1929	2.99	73.5	5.6

[1] From: *Moody's Transportation Manual* (New York: Moody's Investors Service, Inc., 1981).

[2] Estimated by proportion from fragmentary data on trip lengths in F. W. Doolittle, *Studies in the Cost of Urban Transportation Service* (New York: American Electric Railway Association, 1916); Harold Barger, *The Transportation Industries, 1889–1946* (New York: National Bureau of Economic Research, 1951).

[3] Computed based on data in notes 1 and 2.

TABLE 2-5 Postulated Change in the Temporal
Composition of Street Railway Ridership,
1922–1927

Market Segment:	Percentage Change:
Weekday peak	+15%
Weekday off peak	−10
Saturday peak	+10
Saturday off peak	−10
Holiday and Sunday excursion travel	−30
Total	−3

Sources: Fragmentary data in Edward S. Mason,
The Street Railway in Massachusetts (Cam-
bridge, Mass.: Harvard University Press, 1932);
Emerson P. Schmidt, *Industrial Relations in
Urban Transportation* (Minneapolis: University
of Minnesota Press, 1937); and The American
Electric Railway Association, *Electric Railway
Operations in 1925* (New York: AERA, 1926).

beat back the competition of the automobile. But with off-peak ridership and revenues in decline, extending service only compounded
transit's financial difficulties.[8]

The importance of weekend and off-peak ridership to transit's
financial viability can be gauged from Table 2-6. It shows a temporally
disaggregated balance sheet for a "typical" large-city transit operation
circa 1920. The property's profitability hinges on a stable volume of
off-peak traffic because serving this market segment produces 72 percent of the property's revenues but occasions only 63 percent of its
operating costs. In contrast, peak-period operations account for only
28 percent of the property's revenues but occasion 37 percent of its

TABLE 2-6 A Temporal Disaggregation of a "Typical"
Street Railway's Operating Revenues and Expenses

	Four Peak Hours	Residual 20 Hours	All 24 Hours
Percentage of revenues attributable to peak and off-peak period	28%	72%	100%
Percentage of costs occasioned by peak and off-peak operations	37	63	100

Source: F. W. Doolittle, *Studies in the Cost of Urban Transportation
Service* (New York: American Electric Railway Association, 1916).

total operating expenses. The property's financial position would be seriously compromised if off-peak ridership declined and commuter ridership increased. A decline in off-peak ridership would erode the property's revenues, whereas increasing peak-hour ridership would oblige the property to increase service and shoulder additional cost. If commuter ridership increased while off-peak ridership declined, the property in our example would find itself in the seemingly anomalous position of reporting net ridership growth and net revenue erosion. This is precisely the financial dilemma experienced by big-city street railways in the 1920s.[9] Their financial position was progressively weakened by the loss of off-peak ridership, while the growth of peak-hour ridership effectively foreclosed the option of shedding service to reduce cost. From this brief exposition, it should be evident that off-peak ridership was *absolutely essential* to the profitability of the transit industry and that its selective loss deprived transit of the revenue to counterbalance the costs incurred in serving the rush-hour peak.

The financial difficulties created by the erosion of weekend and midday ridership were compounded by the loss of seasonal patronage— patronage associated with Christmas shopping and summer-evening excursions. These markets were extraordinarily important to an industry burdened by as heavy fixed costs as street railways were. Indeed, year-to-year profitability hinged on the state of the economy and the inclination of consumers to spend or save at Christmas time. Just as the profitability of modern department stores turns on holiday-season sales, the financial fortunes of transit properties in the 1920s were closely linked to the ebb and flow of holiday traffic. Street railways could pay dividends in good years when downtowns bustled with Christmas shoppers, but the same property might generate no return for investors in a lean year when consumers guarded their savings. Such were the margins on which many properties operated.

Unfortunately for the industry, holiday traffic proved particularly vulnerable to the competition of the automobile and declined steadily from the 1920s onward. Indeed, seasonal patronage variation has become a burden for the modern industry because winter blizzard conditions accentuate the requirements for rush-hour capacity and thus compound the peak-hour cost problem in the cities of the frostbelt.

PATRONAGE TRENDS SINCE THE 1920s

The selective erosion of patronage that began in the 1920s resumed after World War II. The resulting change in the composition of transit's

TABLE 2-7 Estimated Change in Transit Traffic
by Submarket, 1926 Peak to 1972 Trough*

Market Segment:	Percentage Change:
Peak period	−30%
With flow direction	−5
Counterflow	−80
Weekday off-peak	−60
Saturday	−80
Sundays and holidays	−85

*Estimated from fragmentary data available for
individual properties.

traffic base is shown in Table 2-7. These estimates are crude approximations based on isolated shards of data. No industrywide data series is available to verify them systematically, but veteran industry leaders attest that they square with their experience.

The dynamic that underlies Table 2-7 is an important one: the transformation of mass transit from an all-purpose transportation utility patronized by persons of all ages and incomes to its present role as a subordinate and supplemental form of transportation that is used primarily by downtown commuters and those who are disadvantaged by aging, poverty, or carelessness.

We can begin to understand the workings of this dynamic by closer examination of those segments of the travel market that transit has lost and those it has retained. They are described qualitatively in Table 2-8. As it suggests, no simple or solitary explanation—the diffusion of the automobile, the development of the suburbs, or the imbalance of public policy—is sufficient to explain the complex dynamics of declining ridership.

With loss of ridership and *particularly with unbalanced loss of ridership* came increasingly grave financial distress. This dynamic began with the initial diffusion of the automobile and continued with renewed force following World War II. The precipitous loss of ridership in the off-peak or "base" period goes a long way toward explaining why transit's financial position deteriorated progressively in both the 1920s and the years following World War II. But it does not explain why transit was unable to respond to the competition of the automobile, reorganize its service offerings, and achieve financial stability and renewed growth. To understand why transit was unable to adjust and recoup, we must understand the industry's developmental history, its operating customs, its labor relations, and its captive relationship to big-city politics.

TABLE 2-8 The Changing Composition of Transit Traffic,
1926 Peak to 1972 Trough

Peak period work trips, with flow direction	Volume was essentially stable in larger cities but was concentrated in a narrower peak due to the standardization of the workday at eight hours and quitting time at 5:00 P.M.
Peak period work trips, counterflow direction	The directional split was 65:35 early in the 1950s; a ratio of 90:10 is more typical today.
Short-distance trips	These riders were discouraged by the sharply increasing fares that followed both World War I and World War II. Route attenuation and increasing congestion reduced the level of service afforded the short-distance rider. Market base was reduced by the decline of central-city population in the 1950s and 1960s.
Swing- and night-shift work trips	This market eroded by the relocation of manufacturing activities that followed World War II.
Saturday work trips	This major transit market was reduced sharply by the adoption of the five-day work week following the depression.
Excursion travel	Primarily group travel, this market, a major one during the first two decades of the century, was decimated by the diffusion of the automobile in the 1920s and 1950s.
School trips	This was diverted to yellow buses in many school districts; it was also eroded by the decline of the school-age population in central cities.
Night-on-the-town traffic	Primarily group travel, this was rapidly diverted to the automobile, compounded by the decline of urban entertainment districts and the diffusion of radio and television.
The butcher and baker trade; the rider with the twine-handled shopping bag	This segment was displaced by "the convenience triad": the automobile, supermarket, and home refrigerator.
The Saturday garment and millinery trade	This major market through the 1940s was eroded by decline of downtain retailing and the competition of suburban shopping centers and boutiques.
Weekday window shopping; the matinee market	This was a major midday and summer-evening market until the depression. Primarily group travel and thus readily diverted to auto, the decline was compounded by change in the racial composition of central cities, racial barriers, and the limited buying power of black households.

Transit's developmental history will be explored in the next chapter; for now, we are content to conclude that

1. Gradual decline has been the secular trend of the transit industry for more than 50 years.
2. The true crest of ridership was reached in the 1920s.
3. Ridership levels recorded during World War II and the postwar normalization period did not reflect the demand for transit service that would have prevailed under conditions of stable peacetime employment.
4. The wartime peak was an artificial one and the precipitous decline of patronage following World War II represented a return to normalcy.
5. Transit's distress was compounded by postwar highway, land-use, and housing policies, but the root causes of decline are much more deeply imbedded in the history and structure of the industry, and the inadequacy of its response to social and demographic change.

NOTES

1. This is the central argument of J. R. Meyer, J. F. Kain, and M. Wohl, *The Urban Transportation Problem* (Cambridge, Mass.: Harvard University Press, 1965). For an elegant summation of this view, see George W. Hilton, "The Urban Mass Transportation Assistance Program," in James C. Miller III, ed., *Perspectives on Federal Transportation Policy* (Washington, D.C.: American Enterprise Institute, 1975), p. 131.

2. This argument is made with the greatest sophistication in George M. Smerk, *Urban Transportation: The Federal Role* (Bloomington: Indiana University Press, 1965), pp. 31-57.

3. See especially Lyle C. Fitch, *Urban Transportation and Public Policy* (San Francisco: Chandler, 1964).

4. Charles Stephenson, *Transit's Prospects for Postwar Traffic* (New York: American Transit Association, 1944), p. 7.

5. Association of American Railroads, *Economic and Transportation Prospects* (New York: AAR, 1946), p. 73.

6. Subcommittee on Housing, Senate Banking and Currency Committee, *Hearings on S. 345* (Washington, D.C.: Government Printing Office, 1961), p. 372.

7. American Electric Railway Association, *Electric Railway Operations in 1925* (New York: AERA, 1926), p. 5.

8. R. H. Pinkley, "How the Industry Is Progressing," *Proceedings, 1927,* Annual Convention of the American Electric Railway Association (New York: AERA, 1927), pp. 127-129.

9. Emerson P. Schmidt, *Industrial Relations in Urban Transportation* (Minneapolis: University of Minnesota Press, 1937), pp. 71-74.

3

TRANSIT'S GROWTH AND DECLINE— A PLAY IN EIGHT ACTS

INTRODUCTION

This chapter will sketch the history of transit's growth and decline. Our intent is to weave a story that captures the main threads of the industry's development and subsequent distress. Much like a play with eight acts, the history of mass transit can be divided into epochs, each characterized by a distinctive dynamic:

The horsecar era	1855–1890
Electrification and explosive growth	1890–1906
The era of punitive regulation	1906–1916
The era of wartime intervention	1917–1919
Transition from distress to decline	1920–1929
The buffeting of depression and war	1930–1946
The era of precipitous decline	1947–1960
The period of recovery without stabilization	1961–1980

THE HORSECAR ERA

Writing in 1898, Charles Francis Adams observed that

> The street railway [is] ... an improved line of omnibuses, running over a special pavement. The analogy throughout is with the omnibus line, and

not with the railroad train; with the public thoroughfare and not with the private right of way.[1]

As Adams's commentary suggests, urban mass transit is the lineal descendant of the horsedrawn trolley. The public transit properties of today operate with a fare structure, a route structure, a merchandising philosophy, and a legacy of labor militancy inherited from the days of the horsecar. The conventions and idioms of the industry were molded in the years following the Civil War when only nine cities had populations in excess of 100,000 and the reach of urban development was limited by the endurance of horses and the plodding speed of horse and car.

Many horsecar lines were promotions conceived by local merchants and venture capitalists with a stake in the development of real estate or the stimulation of trade.[2] The capital required for such promotion was modest because tracks were overlaid on city streets, and thus land acquisition did not factor in the cost of entry. Because financing was within the reach of local merchants and venture capitalists, the industry developed in the entrepreneurial format of private ownership. Because tracks were laid over public rights-of-way, the industry was regulated by franchise or charter obligations from its beginnings. And because franchises conferred exclusive territorial rights, monopoly was vested as an entitlement of ownership. Private ownership and territorial monopoly combined to shape the industry's basic structure and traditions:

Horsecars were operated by wage labor rather than owner-operators as had been the norm for the trackless carriage.

Competition was primarily but not exclusively limited to rivalries for territorial privilege.

The governmental favor that was necessary to secure franchises and ensure their renewal entangled properties in electoral politics and political obligations.

Fares were fixed by perpetual convenant to prevent the abuse of monopoly power. Convenants adopted during the 1880s set fares at 5 cents.[3]

The horsecar promoters of the 1880s did not view a fixed 5 cent fare as a particularly burdensome limitation. Most properties were able to earn handsome returns with a 5 cent fare, and with the general price level falling, inflation was neither problematic nor anticipated.[4] Indeed, many promoters sought a fixed fare so as to insulate their operations from political pressures for fare reduction. But, as a consequence, riders came to view a constant fare as a rightful entitlement.

Other customs and conventions of the transit industry are also artifacts of the era of the horsedrawn trolley. The two-man crew that prevailed as the industry norm through the 1920s and into the 1930s is attributable to the demanding role of the teamster. Handling horses and collecting fares was a job for two men in the era of horsepower; it continued by custom and contract guarantee in the period of electric traction. Indeed, some street railways converted to bus operations as the only pragmatic way to eliminate the cost of two-man crews.

The industry's characteristically adversarial labor-management relations also date to the horsepower period.[5] The industry frequently hired immigrant labor, and many owners treated their workers with contempt, paid them poorly, and worked them 14 to 16 hours a day, seven days a week. Abuse and exploitation were so undisguised and so universal that street railwaymen were among the first industrial workers to organize a national union.[6] By 1910, the street railway industry ranked with the garment trade, mining, and railroading as the nation's most thoroughly organized industries. In that year, 24 percent of the industry's work force was unionized compared with 11 percent in manufacturing.[7]

The flat fare—uniform regardless of the distance traveled—is another artifact of the horsedrawn period. It was appropriate to horsecar routes that averaged little more than 3 miles in length. Merchandising fares that allow commuters to purchase tokens or ticket books at a discount rate also date to the same period. Some properties adopted them to stimulate ridership among lower-paid workers who would otherwise have walked to work; other properties were forced to adopt them during episodes of conflict with city government.[8] Thus, by custom, riders came to expect that travel during the peak period should be priced at a reduced—or commuted—rate.

By 1890, the peak of the horsecar era, the industry carried 2 billion passengers annually, employed more than 70,000 workers, and generated operating revenues of approximately $100 million, paying dividends equivalent to 11 percent of gross income.[9]

ELECTRIFICATION AND EXPLOSIVE GROWTH

Technological advances in the generation and transmission of electricity permitted the electrification of street railways during the 1890s. In turn, electrification allowed railway companies to operate larger vehicles at higher speeds over longer routes.

With electrification came the extension of routes, the introduction of service in cities and towns previously unserved by street railways, and the consolidation of rival properties into larger, sometimes city-wide, syndicates. Many properties retailed electricity as well as transportation and were the forebearers of consolidated electric utility companies. Track mileage trebled from 1890 to 1902, while the number of coaches in service almost doubled.[10]

Table 3-1 shows the dramatic expansion of the industry in terms of trackage, fleet size, ridership, markets served, and debt load. This explosive development was fostered by a kind of bandwagon psychology on the part of both investors and local communities.[11] Civic boosters in local communities saw streetcar service as an agent of economic development—physical evidence that their community was a member of the "growth club" of towns and cities of economic importance. As a result, franchises conferring monopoly rights were granted to street railway promoters without pause in many cities and states. Investors displayed a similar inclination to view electrification as a windfall investment opportunity. Investors may have shown less than customary caution because

Franchise monopoly privileges were interpreted as a guarantee of sure future earnings.

Fixed fares were seen as a promise of extraordinary returns because it was expected that electrification would permit significant reduction in street railway operating costs.

TABLE 3-1 The Street Railway Industry, 1890 and 1902

	1890	1902
Trackage (in miles)	5,783	16,652
Electrified trackage	914	16,230
Coaches	32,505	60,290
Fares paid (in 1000s)	2,023,010	4,774,212
Number of properties	789	987
Passengers per mile of track	249,047	212,217
Debt payments as a percentage of gross income	2.8%	10.2%
Dividend payments as a percentage of gross income	11.1%	6.3%

Source: U.S. Census Bureau, Street and Electric Railways, 1902 (Washington, D.C.: Government Printing Office, 1905).

The superior speed and reach of the electric railway promised increases in future patronage and future revenues as urban populations grew and routes were extended to serve new development. Promoters promised that consolidation of small horse railways into larger traction syndicates would produce economies of scale in management, power generation, and operation, permitting the rationalization of service in a fashion that would simultaneously reduce costs and attract new patronage.

Windfall profits *were* made in the boom period of electrification and street railway expansion, but these typically accrued to promoters who secured franchise rights, arranged debt financing, sold securities, provided construction oversight, and, in many cases, speculated in joint promotion of real estate and streetcar lines. Thus, some electrification ventures created enormous wealth—but for the promoters and syndicators for system development rather than for the operating companies and their shareholders that assumed ownership after construction.[12]

As a representative of the Electric Street Railway Association, the industry's trade group, later told a federal board of inquiry,

> Large fortunes were made. They were made, however, out of capitalizing (the street railway's) future and selling the securities, and not out of the five-cent fare rider. The five-cent fare never produced more than a fair return upon the fair investment of the property, but hopes were capitalized, and hopes were sold, and the [second generation of] investors have lost money.[13]

A promoter of street railway development told the same board of inquiry how windfall profits could be made:

> Now the one thing that was uppermost in my mind always was the franchise; I wanted to be sure that there was a 5-cent fare in the franchise, and that I had a franchise for as long term as possible. I have repeatedly refused to be interested in street railway propositions that did not embody a 5-cent fare and a long-term franchise. This franchise gives an enormous value to the property, over and above its physical worth.

> The bankers were keen to see that.

> Taking advantage of the situation, we commenced to capitalize the earning power, because we had a monopoly. If we did not have a monopoly, we went on and bought the other road, and put them together as a basis of some additional capitalization.

> The result was that it was about as lucrative a business as there was in this country in the early stage of the game, and the securities became very desirable, became generally distributed, and, next to steam railroad securi-

ties, were the most popular form of investment on the part of the general public.[14]

The actual earnings of most operating companies proved far more modest than the expectations on which the streetcar development boom was premised. The rapid expansion of the 1890s produced an industry composed of a handful of very profitable firms, a larger number of marginally profitable firms, and a preponderance of firms unable to generate sufficient earnings to pay any return on capital invested in their common stock.[15]

In many instances, local investors with a civic booster's confidence in their community's growth potential were left holding worthless securities when passenger revenues proved insufficient to pay even the out-of-pocket cost of streetcar operation.[16] In other instances, properties were marginally profitable but unable to weather the down cycles of the economy that periodically depressed ridership and revenues. In still other instances, properties were able to establish a modest earnings record—but only after entering receivership for the purpose of shedding service and restructuring their finances.

While stock watering seems to have been the norm, many old-line horsecar companies pursued a policy of conservative capitalization and gradual expansion. These properties approached electrification on a line-by-line basis, capitalizing the introduction of the new technology out of retained earnings. These companies served prime urban markets with an already established riding habit and higher than average traffic densities. This class of property dominated the industry in terms of ridership and real physical assets, although the absolute number of such properties was relatively small.

Under franchise arrangements, these properties were not immune from competition if a rival syndicate could arrange to obtain franchise rights to offer service on a parallel route.[17] Where traffic densities were high, promotions of competitive operations occurred frequently. This forced established companies to respond preemptively—expanding service to preempt the entry of a competing property and avoid the ruinous division of traffic with a competitor franchised to operate a parallel route. The result was the creation of route network more dense than could be justified by its revenue potential. Thus, even conservatively managed and capitalized companies were gradually weakened by overinvestment in physical plant and the acquisition of competing properties.

Soundly financed companies were also damaged by the disorderly market in street railway securities that resulted from speculative promotions and overcapitalization. As investors lost confidence in street railway securities, the stock values and credit ratings of even the most soundly managed properties were damaged by association.[18]

We can summarize the street railway development boom of the 1890s by reemphasizing that it was based on outsized expectations that led to overcapitalization of future earnings and the overexpansion of physical facilities. This was an extraordinarily important period in the industry's development because it damaged investor confidence in street railways and impaired the credit of even the most conservatively capitalized properties.

It also served to poison relations between local government and operating properties. The inflated promises made for street railway investments and the conspicuous fortunes made by promotional syndicates created the impression that operating properties were reaping windfall profits. In turn, the presumption of excess profits led to an extended period of adversary relations between street railways and local officials.

THE ERA OF PUNITIVE REGULATION

A monopoly widely perceived to be reaping windfall profits, street railways became a conspicuous target of campaign oratory and adverse newspaper editorializing during the first decade of the twentieth century.[19] Inadequacies of service—crush loads during the peak hour, infrequent service during evening hours, poorly ventilated coaches— were interpreted as exploitive profiteering and callous abuse of monopoly power. The failure to provide service that would meet a high standard of public comfort and convenience was interpreted as exploitation rather than as evidence of limited earning power.

This impression was reinforced by trends in the ownership of traction companies—the increase in horizontal integration, syndicate ownership, and elaborate pyramid financing schemes that occurred in the first decade of the twentieth century.[20]

The relations between operating properties and local government deteriorated further as weak companies with depressed stock values were absorbed into larger traction syndicates owned by trusts and holding companies searching for low-cost acquisitions that would allow them to issue additional stock in the parent organization at comparatively high face values. Acquisition of local properties by holding companies entailed absentee ownership, a factor that further damaged relations between operations management and local officeholders. Thus, street railways became embroiled in the dominant political currents of the Progressive Era: antagonism to the maneuvers of "trusts" and "giant corporations," opposition to syndicate control, and legislation to regulate public utilities. As the trade association that represented street railways later conceded, the public repute of the industry was badly damaged by the excesses associated first with promotion and then syndicate financing:

> The average man's mind is filled with the suspicion and prejudice that are the outgrowth of evils associated with the promotional stage of street railways of 25 or 30 years ago, when they were in a boom period; when no provision for their regulation as public utilities had been made and when the rapid development of a new and little understood business resulted in evils which are today condemned by responsible managements as well as the public.[21]

By 1907, it was popular wisdom that street railways were offering inadequate service at a monopoly price that was earning excess profits for absentee owners. This led to franchise amendments and tax levies that can be characterized accurately as reprisals, although they were proposed as reforms. Franchise guarantees afforded properties only partial immunity from these reforms. Opportunities to revise or renegotiate franchise obligations actually presented themselves frequently: at the time of franchise renewal, or when rival investment groups proposed a competing franchise, or when the property sought relief from its obligation to operate at a fixed 5 cent fare; on occasions requiring approval of changes in ownership or service configuration; or in the negotiating situations created when local government proposed levying special taxes as a bargaining ploy to reopen the question of franchise obligations.

The general public's perception that profits were excessive and service inadequate made the renegotiation of franchise obligations a viable campaign issue and a popular political stance, and by 1910, many of the relatively permissive franchises granted in the 1890s had been thoroughly revised by incremental concessions.

The most important concessions to which properties acceded were[22]

Wider use of discount ticket books—a practice that effectively reduced fares for regular users and reinforced the perception that wage earners making "necessity trips" have a right to expect discount fares

Free transfer privileges

The transportation of municipal employees at no fare

The extension of service into newly urbanized territory as urban development proceeded—a practice that increased the length of trip served for the 5 cent fare and ingrained the expectation that flat fares are a public right

Increases in the frequency of night service—an obligation that increased operating expenses

Increases in the capacity afforded during rush hours to meet standards of comfort and crowding—an obligation that increased both operating and capital costs.

The frequency of political pressure for concessions on fares and service levels led the industry to embrace state regulation as an alternative to repetitive renegotiation in the municipal political arena. By the advent of World War I, the most important properties had been placed under the regulatory control of state public utility or public service commissions, an arrangement that afforded more insulation from reforms, especially reforms motivated by personal political ambition.

Although it was short-lived, the era of reform and reprisal left a lasting imprint on the industry's fare structure and its service obligations. The concessions made during this period increased both operating and capital costs and reduced the revenue derived from the average passenger. The impact on net earning was significant but not visibly punishing, because the first decade of the twentieth century was characterized by significant increases in ridership.[23] The increase in ridership during this period is attributable to the growth of urban population and to the general prosperity of the period. General economic prosperity contributed especially to an increase in Saturday and Sunday excursion trips and holiday season shopping trips.

During the same period, the larger urban properties realized operating economies by replacing the first generation of trolley coaches with larger vehicles capable of accelerating faster and carrying more passengers. The speed and capacity of the new equipment allowed properties to increase the seat miles of service provided without increasing the size of their labor force or coach fleet. At the time, it was not anticipated that the new, heavier vehicles would result in a significant increase in the cost of track maintenance and replacement. The difficulty of anticipating such costs, the consequent inadequacy of depreciation reserves, and the loss of depreciation due to premature obsolescence played an important role in impairing the earning power of the industry throughout its developmental period.[24] During the first years of its operation, new equipment allowed considerable economy of operation, and it combined with urban population growth and the growth of off-peak excursion travel to mask the cost of fare and service concessions.

Because the cost of fare and service concessions was offset by ridership growth and operating economies, they were not bitterly contested by the industry. As a consequence, the fare concessions and service standards adopted in the era of reform as a forced concession became established as continuing public service obligation and eventually assumed the stature of a vested social right.

Industry Composition

To explain the effects of reform-era regulation on street railway development, we must understand the composition and structure of the industry in the first decade of the twentieth century. By 1907, the period of explosive growth ignited by the development of electric motive power had run its course.[25] Installed capacity was sufficient to match traffic volume in most markets, and excess capacity was evident in many thin markets. Thus, service in place was sufficient to serve existing urban population, and the growth potential of the industry hinged on future population growth. The rate of population growth was sufficient to require significant new investment from year to year in the larger urban markets, but the growth of revenue patronage that could be expected to result from additional investment was lower than in the developmental years of the industry.

During the developmental period 1890 to 1907, the number of operating firms in the industry had increased from 769 to 945.[26] Many of the newer firms entering the business during the boom years of electrification were properties that supplemented passenger revenues with the sale of electric current; their economic base was thus a compound of transportation, light, and power sales.[27] As we have noted, street railway operations provided the economic base that begot many of today's electric utilities.

Through merger, acquisition, and the pyramiding of stock ownership, the distinction between the old-line street railways and the newer consolidated utilities was blurred over time. By 1907, a sizable fraction of the large and midsized urban markets were served by consolidated utilities that sold both transportation and electricity.[28] At least one-third and perhaps as many as half of the operating properties could be classified as consolidated light, power, and traction utilities by 1907.

The consolidated utility provided an extraordinarily efficient mechanism for the diversion of earnings from street railway reinvestment to the expansion of light and power operations. Diversion of earnings seems to have become the norm as general inflation combined with the fixed 5 cent fare and punitive regulations to impair the earning power of street railways.[29]

During the "reform" era, the technology necessary for generating and transmitting electricity was developing at an extraordinary pace, as were technologies and products based on the consumption of electricity.[30] The light and power industry was poised, in short, for a surge of growth much like the one that had propelled street railway expansion a decade earlier. With fare and service concessions compounding the differential in the returns that could be earned from investments in street railways and electric utilities, many consolidated utilities shifted their investment priorities. The result was a sharp reduction in new street railway investment, a reduction in dividend payments, and further damage to the reputation of street railway securities, including those of companies engaged solely in the provision of transportation.

Much the same phenomenon was occurring in the capital markets. Investors seeking safe returns from public utility stocks and bonds shunned street railway issues and shifted capital to the safer haven of light and power companies. This trend was accelerated by the emergence of the municipal ownership movement and the first proposals for the condemnation of transit properties and their operation in public ownership. Table 3-2 shows the pattern of investment in street railways and steam-generating facilities from 1900 to World War I. It shows that 1907 was the high-water mark for street railway investment and that 1908 was a year of surging investment in light and power facilities. Not coincidentally, 1907 was a year of panic in the equity markets—a shake-

TABLE 3-2   Gross Capital Expenditures for Street Railways
and Electric Utilities, 1900–1917
(in millions of 1929 constant dollars)

Year	Street Railway Investment	Electric Utility Investment
1900	$258.9	$119.6
1901	269.9	165.9
1902	280.2	197.3
1903	300.0	202.7
1904	328.2	217.2
1905	342.9	234.1
1906	343.5	250.8
1907	355.6	269.4
1908	234.5	351.7
1909	144.6	382.8
1910	209.1	417.7
1911	177.3	454.5
1912	128.3	493.9
1913	163.8	288.5
1914	159.3	292.3
1915	164.8	234.2
1916	117.7	230.6
1917	144.9	358.5

Source: Melvile J. Ulmer, *Capital in Transportation, Communications and Public Utilities* (Princeton, N.J.: Princeton University Press, 1960).

out year in which stock values plunged, although not as dramatically as during the crash of 1929.

Investor confidence in street railway securities had been virtually destroyed by 1912, and a pattern of net disinvestment is evident after 1916.[31] After 1916, the assets of street railways were being used up faster than they were being replaced through reinvestment. As a consequence, track mileage peaked in 1917 and declined thereafter.[32]

Street railways lost investor confidence because of the profiteering of early street railway promoters and the overcapitalization they fostered. This was compounded by the punitive response of local governments that used fare and service regulations to attach for their constituents what were perceived as excess profits. At the same time, operating costs were increasing due to both general inflation and the damaged risk rating of railway debt. Thus, even before World War I, street railways were a troubled industry with damaged financial standing and suspect earning power.[33]

The ability of large and midsized properties to meet operating expenses from operating revenues was not at issue or in doubt during this period. What had become problematic was the industry's ability to generate income sufficient to reward past investment and secure future capital in competition with other investment opportunities.

As the nation readied for war, the investment situation was one that gravely concerned street railway owners and managers.[34] What they did not anticipate at the time was that the industry's ability to meet even operating expenses was based on the shakiest of foundations.

WARTIME INTERVENTION

The operating profitability of street railways rested on a foundation of low wages and extended working hours.[35] These conditions could be sustained as long as most street railway workers remained unorganized and the ranks of the blue-collar labor force were being swelled by the massive volume of immigration that characterized the industry's developmental years. World War I marked an abrupt change in the circumstances that had allowed and sustained the exploitation of labor.

The wage rates paid by street railways at the turn of the century were influenced by two dominant but countervailing factors. On the one hand, the skills required for the work of motormen and conductors were relatively modest. Since little special training was required, street railways could employ from the large pool of general laborers, and, since labor costs were the most significant element of operating expense, management had strong incentive to pay the lowest possible wage by hiring at the bottom of the skills ladder.

On the other hand, street railways required a dependable labor force—because company revenues were handled by employees in the form of cash fares, because the company was liable for claims arising from accidents, and because the company's customer relations and public image were highly dependent on the reliability and on the courtesy of its operating personnel. Since street railway working conditions were unattractive, inducing better motivated workers to accept the long hours, the hazard of accidents, and the exposure to inclement weather would normally have required a compensatory pay premium. The heavy migration of the period, however, created a buyer's market for general laborers and allowed street railways to attract moderately skilled workers without paying premium wages.

During the period 1900 to 1917, transit wage rates were established at levels competitive with the pay of moderately skilled workers in manufacturing. Street railway wages floated at an average of 95 percent of the annual wages of manufacturing workers.[36] While the *annual* wages of street railway and manufacturing workers were roughly comparable in 1900, street railway motormen and conductors worked considerably longer hours—often as long as 14 hours a day, six days a week. Thus, the true hourly rate of compensation floated at only 70 to 75 percent of manufacturing wages.

Labor surpluses attributable to migration from Europe and from the farms to the cities allowed street railways to hire at differential wages, but *retaining* dependable workers was another matter. The best available evidence suggests that this was a high-turnover, low-morale industry in which labor was overworked and underpaid.[37] Such was the state of street railway labor relations at the outbreak of World War I.

Labor Relations During World War I

The wartime period was characterized by virulent inflation, which drove consumer prices upward from an index value of 100 in 1916 to 138 in 1918 and 183 in 1920.[38] Rising prices, in turn, led to economy-wide demands for wage adjustment—and threatened to lead to strikes that would disrupt war production.

To avoid labor unrest and work stoppages, President Wilson established a National War Labor Board (NWLB) empowered to arbitrate labor disputes and set impartial, third-party wage guidelines after conducting hearings on a case-by-case basis.[39] President Wilson created the NWLB by executive order in 1918 and instructed it to "secure settlement(s) by local mediation and conciliation."[40] More important, the president's order enunciated a set of principles and policies to guide the board. The president's order

1. affirmed the right of employees to organize in labor unions;
2. affirmed the right of all workers to a living wage, a wage sufficient to "insure the subsistence of the worker and his family in health and reasonable comfort";
3. affirmed the right of women to equal pay for equal work;
4. proposed parity of wage rates and working conditions for comparably skilled workers as a broad guideline for adjustments in compensation; and
5. proposed adoption of the eight-hour day as the standard against which to commensurate rates of pay.[41]

While its findings and recommendations were precatory and not binding, the War Labor Board had significant impact on both the wages and work rules of the street railway industry. Arbitral determinations were made for virtually every major street railway operation in the nation—over 200 in all.[42] The board's findings and awards directly affected 90,500 street railway workers, or almost 60 percent of the industry's labor force.

The War Labor Board adjusted wages upward to compensate for the effects of inflation, but more important, it made additional awards over and above inflation adjustment to bring street railway wages into closer correspondence with those in manufacturing. The decisions of the NWLB increased wages an average of 61 percent, compressed the time schedule of promotions, equalized the wages of men and women performing the same work, and mandated bonus payments for the extended work hours typical of street railway operation.[43]

The rulings of the War Labor Board were based on an equity standard and were made without reference to the industry's earning power. By 1919, street railway wages averaged $1,387 annually as compared with $1,384 in manufacturing—nearly perfect wage parity.[44] As the chairman of the War Labor Board, former president William Howard Taft, explained,

We have found the streetcar men underpaid everywhere . . . and the general range of our rulings has been to bring them up . . .

The financial conditions of the companies had actually in the past kept down wages of the men quite below the wages that were paid in fields of labor of a kindred nature. . . . We had no hesitation in reaching the conclusion that labor was as much entitled to an independent consideration of what its wages should be as a coal man who had furnished coal or a material man who furnished iron; that the question must be determined by what was being paid in similar fields of labor. Therefore, we refused flatly from the first to consider the financial condition of any company in determining the rate of wages.[45]

TABLE 3-3 Indices of Transit
Fares and Wages, 1916–1920
(1916 = 100)

Year	Fares	Wages
1916	100	100
1917	100	108
1918	106	126
1919	121	155
1920	137	194

Source: Edward S. Mason, *The
Street Railway in Massachusetts* (Cambridge, Mass.: Harvard University Press, 1932).

The rulings of the War Labor Board precipitated a crisis in street
railway finance because industry revenues were limited by franchise
covenants guaranteeing the 5 cent fare. Table 3-3 compares the trend
of street railway fares and wages from 1916 to 1920. It shows wages
climbing steeply in response to NWLB awards but fares lagging significantly as most localities ignored the board's entreaties to allow compensatory increases in fares. From 1917 to 1920, operating revenues
increased 40 percent whereas street railway operating expenses increased by almost 70 percent.[46]

The cost-revenue squeeze that resulted from the decisions of the
War Labor Board can be seen in the rapid deterioration of the industry's "operating ratio"—the ratio of operating expenses to operating
revenues. In 1912, the aggregate, industrywide operating ratio stood
at .60. By 1920, it had deteriorated to .78.[47] Table 3-4 shows the trend
for the wartime period.

TABLE 3-4 The Cost-Revenue
Squeeze in Street Railway
Finance, 1912–1920

Year	Operating Ratio
1912	.60
1917	.65
1918	.73
1919	.76
1920	.78

Source: American Electric Rail-
way Association, *The Urban
Transportation Problem* (New
York: AERA, circa 1933).

The most obvious effects of wartime arbitration and inflation can be seen in the demise of smaller properties and in the weakening of the financial position of midsized operations,[48] but the rulings of the War Labor Board also sheltered and fostered union organizing efforts in the street railway industry. In 1920, 24 percent of street railway labor was organized; by war's end, a full 50 percent of the industry's labor force was unionized, compared with only 22 percent in the manufacturing sector.[49] Thus, by 1920, street railways ranked among the most heavily unionized industries with a level of union membership comparable to that found in mining and railroading. Unionization laid the groundwork for continuing upward pressure on street railway wages and operating expenses, compounding the financial difficulties faced by street railways at war's end.

TRANSITION FROM DISTRESS TO DECLINE

The decade of the 1920s was a hinge period for urban public transportation—the decade in which street railways first lost market share and then market dominance to the private automobile. Unable to expand at the pace of rapid urban growth that occurred during the postwar years, street railways also lost their role as a dominant influence on land-use and urban form. Few street railways were able to raise capital for expansion and, thus, surrendered their influence on the pattern of urban settlement. The automobile occupied the vacuum created by the arrested development of street railways and began remaking the geometry of travel and the pattern of cities early in the decade of the 1920s.

The Automobile Comes of Age

The years from 1908 to 1927 might be characterized as the adolescence of the American automobile industry. During this period, the automobile evolved from a touring and sporting machine into an all-weather utility vehicle. Only 10 percent of the automobiles manufactured in 1920 were closed vehicles susceptible to comfortable use in inclement weather, but, by 1927, 83 percent of all newly manufactured cars were closed-body models.[50] This change in vehicle design combined with the development of all-weather highways to mark the coming age of the automobile. The evolution of the automobile from the Model T prototype to the introduction of Ford's Model A is shown in Table 3-5.

During the 1920s, the growth of household income, the maturation of mass-production techniques, and the development of credit arrangements for trading in used vehicles combined to produce steady

TABLE 3-5 The Evolution of the Automobile:
Timeline of the Transition from a Sporting/Touring Machine
to an All-Weather Utility Vehicle, 1908–1927

Year	Developments in Automotive Marketing and Technology	Closed Vehicles as a Percentage of Those Manufactured
1908	Model T Ford introduced	—
1909	Fabric tops introduced	—
1911	Electric starter introduced	—
1913	Installment financing introduced	—
1916	Hand-operated windshield wipers introduced	—
1919	GMAC (the credit arm of GM) created	10%
1920	First shock absorber	17
1922	Balloon tires introduced	30
1923	Dodge offers all-steel closed body; power-operated windshield wipers	34
1924	Ethyl gasoline	43
1925	Bumpers standard equipment	57
1926	Car heating introduced	72
1927	Ford introduces Model A	83

Source: The Automobile Manufacturers Association, *A Chronicle of the Automotive Industry in America, 1893–1952* (Detroit: AMA, 1953).

reduction in the cost of automobile ownership. Table 3-6 shows the trend of motor vehicle purchase price and operating cost from 1912 to 1935; it also shows, for comparison, the trend of street railway fares.

Significantly, the cost of motoring was declining at just the time street railways were seeking fare increases to offset the cost of wartime labor settlements. The successive fare increases sought by street railways in the early 1920s were not conceived as pricing or marketing strategies but rather as "offset" or "catch-up" allowances necessary to restore operating ratios to the level that prevailed before World War I. They failed to restore the industry's financial stability because of fundamental changes in the street railway's competitive environment—the growth of auto ownership and the introduction of the motorbus. Street railways, in short, were playing "catch up" at just the time that fundamental changes in their marketing strategy, pricing philosophy, and industrial relations would have been necessary to

TABLE 3-6 Transit Fares, Automobile Ownership and Operating Costs,
and the Consumer Price Index, Selected Years, 1912-1935

Year	Motor Vehicle Operating Cost Index[1]	Motor Vehicle Purchase Price Index[2]	Transit Fare Index[3]	Consumer Price Index[4]
1912	100	100	100	100
1920	65	101	137	205
1925	46	70	150	180
1930	37	63	160	171
1935	30	56	162	141

[1] From Automotive Council for War Production, *Automotive War Production* (October 1943).

[2] From Automobile Manufacturers Association, *Automobile Facts and Trends* (New York: AMA, 1936).

[3] American Transit Association, *Transit Journal* (New York: ATA, 1937).

[4] U.S. Census Bureau, *Historical Statistics of the United States* (Washington, D.C.: Government Printing Office, 1976).

adjust to competition from the automobile and from independent motorbus operations.

With the purchase price of automobiles declining steadily and real personal income rising, automobile ownership was within reach of the majority of American households by the middle of the 1920s. Table 3-7 shows the steadily increasing market penetration of the automobile in the years following World War I.

TABLE 3-7 The Growth of Automobile Ownership,
Selected Years, 1910-1929

Year	Ratio of Adult Americans to Auto Registrations	Ratio of Households to Automobile Registrations
1910	113.0:1	44.0:1
1915	25.0:1	10.0:1
1920	7.5:1	3.0:1
1925	3.8:1	1.6:1
1926	3.6:1	1.5:1
1927	3.4:1	1.4:1
1928	3.3:1	1.4:1
1929	3.1:1	1.3:1

Sources: Automobile Manufacturers Association, *Automobile Facts and Trends* (New York: AMA, 1936), and U.S. Census Bureau, *Historical Statistics of the United States* (Washington, D.C.: Government Printing Office, 1976).

The Diverse Dynamics of Decline

Some analysts maintain that the initial decline of street railways should not be attributed to the competition of the automobile. Kornhauser, for example, has argued that "the decline was not, originally, demand-induced. At first, there was no superior technology to which riders or suppliers fled. Rather, the drop in mileage indicates the beginning of large numbers of bankruptcies and failures due to other causes."[51] There is some truth in this argument as evidenced by the failure of marginal properties in small communities. We prefer to emphasize that the process of decline showed significant variation among different classes of street railway operation. In fact, it is possible to distinguish three very different modes of decline: (1) bankruptcy, (2) elective disinvestment, and (3) embattled attrition. We will discuss each in turn.

Bankruptcy. As we have noted, the aggregate nationwide operating ratio of the street railway industry deteriorated from .65 to .78 during the war years, effectively destroying the industry's credit and access to capital. The result was literally disastrous for smaller properties operating in marginal markets entered during the later years of speculative promotion. Aggregate industrywide statistics understate the financial distress of these properties, as Table 3-8 shows. It reveals that many of these properties were beyond financial rescue by war's end.

In 1912, 729 street railways were small operations with annual revenues less than $250,000. By 1917, the number of properties in this class had shrunk to 650 by dint of bankruptcy, merger, or foreclosure

TABLE 3-8 A Disaggregate Portrait of Street Railway Financial Performance: Average Operating Ratio by Size of Property, Selected Years, 1912–1920

Year	Properties with Revenue in Excess of $1 Million	Properties with Revenue in Excess of $250,000 but Less than $1 million	Properties with Revenues of Less than $250,000
1912	.57	.62	.68
1917	.62	.66	.73
1920	.72	.82	.89
Number of properties in this class in 1917	114	179	650

Source: U.S. Census Bureau, *Electric Railways and Affiliated Motor Bus Lines, 1927* (Washington, D.C.: Government Printing Office, 1931).

sale.[52] At war's end, only 508 street railways of this class remained in independent operation. In 1912, they had carried 8 percent of the nation's street railway patrons, but accounted for nearly a quarter of street railway trackage. By 1922, they accounted for less than 4 percent of nationwide patronage and only 15 percent of total trackage. Between 1916 and 1922, 88 of these marginal properties terminated operations without provision for reorganization or replacement.[53] They were destroyed by a combination of factors: wartime increases in wages and prices; maintenance and replacement deferred during the war years; delays in obtaining regulatory approval for fare increases; and exhaustion of credit. The fragile financial foundation of small roads that had weathered the war years was damaged irreparably by the diffusion of the automobile. Indeed, the early diffusion of the automobile was most vigorous in the small farmbelt cities where many of these marginal properties were located.

In these markets, the automobile was rapidly adopted as a substitute for the horse and buggy and the light truck was substituted for the horse and wagon.[54] Almost incidentally, the growth of auto and truck ownership diluted the already thin patronage base of *interurban* street railways that provided ancillary urban service for small-city residents.[55]

Robert and Helen Lynd's exhaustive profile of a "typical" industrial city in Ohio provides a revealing portrait of the place the automobile already occupied in these smaller American cities by 1925:

> The first real automobile appeared in Middletown in 1900. About 1906 it was estimated that "there are probably 200 in the city and county." At the close of 1923 there were 6,221 passenger cars in the city, one for every 6.1 persons, or roughly two for every three families. . . . For some of the workers and some of the business class, use of the automobile is a seasonal matter, but the increase in surfaced roads and in closed cars is rapidly making the car a year-round tool for leisure-time as well as getting-a-living activities. As, at the turn of the century, business class people began to feel apologetic if they did not have a telephone, so ownership of an automobile has now reached the point of being an accepted essential of normal living.

> No one questions the use of the auto for transporting groceries, getting to one's place of work, or the golf course, or in place of the porch for "cooling off after supper," [although there is some labor union concern that now] a factory can draw from workmen within a radius of forty-five miles.[56]

Middletown was not atypical of the midsized farmbelt industrial centers in which the patronage base of street railways was rapidly eroded by the diffusion of the automobile. In the 11 states of the upper Midwest, but excluding the city of Chicago, street railway ridership declined by 17 percent from 1922 to 1927—with a punishing effect on marginal properties in smaller cities.[57] By 1927, most small-city properties were operating at a deficit and would be swept out of business altogether by the depression. In some cities with populations between 25,000 and 50,000, street railways would be replaced by small "Mom and Pop" bus operations, but in most cities of this class, mass transportation would be afforded by the automobile and pickup truck after the 1920s.

Elective Disinvestment.   By 1917, a large percentage of street railway operations were owned by consolidated utilities or controlled by utility trusts through holding companies. The proportion of properties held in this manner was probably close to 50 percent, although it is impossible to arrive at an exact estimate.[58] As we have already noted, properties of this class were diverting railway surplus for the development of steam-generating capacity in the first decade of the twentieth century.[59] Many, but not all, of these same properties pursued a policy of elective disinvestment during the 1920s. In contrast, large properties engaged solely in the business of transportation were increasing service to compete with the automobile. While some consolidated utilities increased service to improve their competitive position, the norm for this class of property seems to have been retrenchment whether by choice or default. The data to support this assertion are suggestive but not conclusive.

We do know with certainty that there were forceful economic incentives for consolidated utilities to emphasize the development of light- and power-generating capability at the expense of reinvestment in street railway operations. From 1917 to 1922, the gross income of light and power companies increased over 100 percent, whereas output increased some 58 percent.[60] Unlike street railways, light and power utilities were able to obtain wartime rate increases, and higher rates accounted for half of the increase in gross income. By contrast, the gross revenues of street railways increased only 44 percent, and, because localities resisted fare increases for street railways, *net* income actually declined 9.3 percent during the period 1917 to 1922.[61]

The development of refrigeration, home appliances, and the use of electricity in manufacturing and industrial heating were simultaneously creating new markets for electric power. The result was an increasingly wide gap in both growth and profit potential between the transportation and power-generating activities of consolidated utilities.

The financial requirements of capitalizing new electric-generating capacity were probably sufficient to exhaust the credit of most utilities and squeeze out street railway investment by default if not design. Indeed, the output of central electric stations doubled in the short span of six years from 1920 to 1926.[62] Given the trend of power sales and the diversity of potential customers, economically rational management would have invested both capital and effort in the profit center with the most significant growth potential—light and power operations.

Unfortunately, the data available to compare the investment behavior of consolidated utilities with that of properties engaged solely in the provision of transportation services are poor at best. The Census of Electrical Industries is the best available source, but its reports were compiled in a fashion that blurs the distinction among consolidated utilities, properties engaged solely in the operation of transit services, and properties with separate capital accounts for street railways and electric utility operations. Table 3-9 shows the most discrete classification that can be accomplished using census data. It *suggests* that consolidated utilities were the properties most actively engaged in disinvestment, but the evidence is far from conclusive.

There is, however, qualitative evidence that supports the thesis that many consolidated utilities were pursuing a policy of elective retrenchment. When consolidated utilities floated new stock offerings, their portfolios frequently emphasized that "this company receives

TABLE 3-9 Comparison of Different Segments of the
Street Railway Industry, 1922–1927

Item	Properties Engaged Solely in the Provision of Mass Transportation or with Separate Accounting Systems for Electric Utility Operations	Consolidated Utilities Selling Both Transportation and Electricity and Keeping Joint Accounts
Revenue passengers	−5.9%	−15.9%
Revenue car miles	+0.3	−17.5
Operating revenues, transportation	+0.4	−22.4
Operating expenses, transportation	+4.3	21.3
Net operating revenues, transportation	−10.7	−26.6

Source: U.S. Census Bureau, *Electric Railways,* 1927 (Washington, D.C.: Government Printing Office, 1931).

only X percent of its revenue from electric railways."[63] Similarly, descriptions of street railway holdings were typically buried in descriptive portfolios even when they accounted for a large percentage of the utility's asset value—evidence that management viewed them as a liability in the financial markets.

The cumulative weight of the evidence argues that many consolidated utilities gave priority to capitalizing electric power operations and suggests that many allowed their street railway operations to decline by default if not design.

Embattled Attrition. Foreclosure, bankruptcy, and elective disinvestment describe the mode of decline of street railways in large numbers, but not that of the industry's most important properties—those in the larger cities.

Larger urban properties made strenuous efforts to recoup from the financial battering suffered during the war years. These properties pursued an aggressive recovery strategy: seeking and obtaining fare increases, shedding costs, extending service, and replacing aging equipment. As we shall see, this class of street railways lost patronage to the automobile in oblique rather than direct competition.

In larger cities—the forebears of today's metropolitan areas—the diffusion of the automobile lagged that in smaller cities. More important, the use of the automobile presented a different kind of competitive challenge to big-city railways than to their small-city counterparts. By 1925, more than half the households in cities with populations of 100,000 or more could be counted among the ranks of the "automobile."[64] In these urban centers, the substitution of auto travel for street railway use was offset by the rapid growth of industrial employment and its correlate, urban population. Just as important, the quality of service afforded by street railways was sufficient to sustain demand for the kind of routine and recurrent travel involved in the journey to work. Properties operating in these markets experienced little erosion of patronage, and many actually recorded increasing commuter ridership during the rush-hour periods.[65]

While total patronage remained reasonably stable, the composition of the typical property's patronage base was changing subtly but dramatically. Midday, excursion, nighttime, and weekend ridership was being lost to the automobile, while commuter ridership was increasing.[66] Indeed, the decline of larger properties was precipitated not by the loss of ridership in general but by the gradual erosion of the off-peak and weekend ridership necessary to counterbalance the high cost of providing capacity sufficient to accommodate the rush-hour peaks.

The financial dilemma posed by increasingly unbalanced load

factors was compounded by pressures to extend and expand service as population growth distended the boundaries of urban settlement. Pressure to extend and expand service was exerted by the residents of the bedroom suburbs that were built up during the housing boom of the 1920s, by commerce associations with a stake in the growth of downtown retailing and fearful of suburban commercial rivalry, and by the emergence of competitive carriers operating independent motorbus service.

The pressure to serve new residential developments and accommodate downtown growth was a millstone of street railway operations from the beginning.[67] That pressure intensified following World War I as postwar prosperity fueled urban growth and new residential development. The resulting friction between street railways and municipal authorities has been described as follows:

> One of the greatest problems that now confronts the electric trolley company is the need of giving service into newly opened sections [of the city]. This is a constant cause of conflict. A new suburb develops. Its residents demand service. The trolley company investigates. It finds that the utmost possible patronage to be gained will not permit an even break on the costs of installing a new line. Either it declines to add a spur to its existing trackage and thereby increases the public resentment against itself, or it establishes such a line and accepts a loss.[68]

Requests for service extension were a source of nearly constant friction between street railways and local authorities because city growth hinged on the access provided by streetcar lines. As a monopoly supplier of transportation, the street railway was obliged to serve new developments in outlying districts—or so local officials argued. But such extensions were undertaken with reluctance because the flat fares typical of street railway operation virtually assured that attenuated routes would diminish the property's overall return on investment. This was particularly true after 1920, when financial institutions began offering installment credit that allowed prospective homebuyers to purchase larger homes on larger lots.

Increasing house and lot size reduced the density of new residential development and, with it, the density of traffic per mile of track and per hour of coach operation. Extending street railway lines to serve these developments was extraordinarily costly because it obliged properties to increase peak-hour labor and equipment so as to maintain acceptable headways and load factors on established route segments. The result was financially destructive: new extensions generated less traffic per coach mile than did established route segments; new extensions obliged properties to pay the high marginal costs associated with additional peak-hour labor and equipment; and they afforded less than average revenue per passenger mile because service was rendered at a flat fare. By 1920, it was evident that "the long haul riders are being carried at a loss and are eating up the net income of the companies."[69]

As a consequence, most properties sought to deflect pressure for service extension by pleading financial distress. Some properties with real estate subsidiaries were able to capture the increase in land values that joint development of housing and streetcar service promised to generate, but this was the exception rather than the rule by the 1920s. Joint development was foreclosed as an option for most properties because their impaired credit standing deprived them access to the capital necessary for real estate development. Instead, most street railways pleaded poverty as their strategy for avoiding unremunerative extensions.

Street Railways and the Motorbus

The emergence of motorbus service operated by competitive independents fundamentally altered the circumstances that had allowed street railways to deflect pressure for service extension. Prior to the introduction of the motorbus, street railways had two options when localities pressed for service extension.[70] They could extend trackage and afford service at a loss, or they could refuse to provide service, hazarding the goodwill of local officials whose support or acquiescence was necessary to obtain fare increases. With the development of the motorbus and its introduction by independent operators, street railway managers were confronted with a larger but equally uncomfortable range of options. They could extend streetcar lines, concede the new territory to an independent operator, or introduce and operate bus service as an adjunct to their streetcar operations.

Most street railways opted to preserve their territorial monopoly and afford bus service that connected with streetcar lines; others were forced to do so by the decisions of public utility commissions. Thus, the entry of street railways into bus operations was primarily preemptive and defensive. Its logic was expressed as follows in 1920:

> Cities will continue to spread out and transportation facilities will be required to serve the new districts. Much growth will occur along lines of existing railways. But other territory will be built up requiring new facilities. Here is [the] place for the motor bus operated as an integral part of the city transportation plant. The motor bus will permit traffic to be built up to the point where the large investment in a rail line may be justified. The bus will thus conserve capital for more attractive uses.
>
> If the motor bus has a part in the scheme of [outlying] district transportation, then it is the duty of the railway to be the first to find its place and put

it to beneficial use. Ill-advised competition may thus be anticipated and the better interests of the public more advantageously served.[71]

A subcommittee of the American Electric Railway Association articulated a similar view in 1923:

> In its last report your Committee stated in substance that there was a field for the economic use of buses to supplement the electric railway service in the cities of this country, either by inaugurating bus service on lines of light traffic, where track reconstruction was the other alternative, or by using buses for extending service into new territory where the expected traffic was not great enough to warrant the investment in tracks for electric railway service.
>
> Your Committee also concluded that for handling mass transportation the electric railway is the most reliable and economical method now known, but that on account of the availability of buses for the special conditions above stated, the electric railways should be alive to the possibilities of bus operation—both in order to handle all the transportation needs of their community and by so doing to prevent wasteful competition by others entering the field due to the electric railways failing to utilize buses where the need for them exists.
>
> The fact that during the past year the number of electric railway companies operating auxiliary bus service has increased from 44 to 95, involving an increase in buses from 300 to 925, proves that an increasing number of street railway companies are finding places where buses can be used to advantage in supplementing their rail service.
>
> Experience has shown that the motor bus amalgamates well with street railway transportation. It decidedly helps in providing a unified service in which the various companies are trying to provide street transportation. The menace of the jitney, although still with us, has grown less. Particularly has it become apparent during the past year that after the street railway has installed motor bus operation the public has come to realize how much more satisfactory is the service than that previously rendered by various irresponsible, poorly organized jitney companies.[72]

Motorbus extensions of street railway lines were frequently deficit operations and almost invariably reduced a street railway's net income. To understand why street railways were unwilling to concede outlying districts to independent motorbus operators, we must examine the perceived threat of jitney and motorbus competition.

The earliest motorbus companies were typically small operations managed as a family business, and driving a bus or jitney was often a moonlighting sideline for persons otherwise employed. Such operations first emerged in the years before World War I. The typical American motorbus company of 1920 owned a fleet of only three coaches and was basically a "Mom and Pop" operation.[73] Driving, maintenance, scheduling, and bookkeeping were family affairs, unencumbered by union agreements, craft specialization, or strict regulatory oversight. Early motorbus operations were also "blissfully immune from taxes, schedules, [charges for] roadway upkeep and fixed fares."[74] As the American Electric Railway Association was told in 1920,

> Bus operators, as a rule, are irresponsible for damages to property and liability to persons. They can get a permit almost without investigation as to their character or as to the need of the bus service.
>
> Buses may start running at seven o'clock in the morning, where the trolley [must] start at five. They may stop at noon, but the trolley [must] continue uninterrupted. During the rush hours, the bus is permitted to reap a harvest by driving up to terminals, waiting rooms, or corners, and taking from the trolley the cream of its profit—the short-haul patron.[75]

The earliest motorbus companies followed one of two prototypes: suburban operations, which provided limousinelike services for a premium 10 cent fare, or urban operations, which competed directly with street railways on the same or parallel routes. Flexible schedules, a premium fare, low overhead costs, and the provision of midday charter or interurban service allowed suburban motorbus companies to operate profitably, and such services proliferated in the period 1920 to 1925. During this period, the patronage of independent motorbus operations increased dramatically—from 200 million passenger trips in 1920 to 895 million in 1925.[76]

The operation of urban service by independent motorbus companies was, in some cases, a product of conflict between street railways and local authorities. In such cases, motorbus competition was invited or encouraged as a *political* strategy for disciplining street railways unable or unwilling to afford quality service. Motorbus companies could operate profitably in competition with street railways if they were allowed to provide selective service and were able to employ part-time labor. Profitability hinged on serving short routes with dense traffic while avoiding obligations to provide evening, nighttime, or early-morning service. Such competition could become "a serious factor militating against the usefulness and prosperity of the electric railway" and street railways argued that it was "manifestly unfair to let a competitor take away the easy, more profitable and fair weather business, but when travel is light or when it is stormy to have this competitor fail to operate and expect the railway to provide the service needed."[77]

The threat of direct competition with motorbus operations and consequently ruinous division of *urban* traffic seems to have been a primary motivation for street railways to preempt the formation of *suburban* motorbus companies. Operating such services allowed street railways to preempt a latent competitor, satisfy demands for service at a lesser capital cost than would have been entailed in rail extension, court the goodwill of city officials, and, at least in theory, build a traffic base that would generate future profits.

Table 3-10 shows the trend of bus patronage during the 1920s and the preemption of the field by street railways that began after 1925. Preemptive expansion and its companion strategy, the acquisition of independent motorbus operations, preserved the street railway's monopoly and hastened the evolution of streetcar companies into mixed-mode transit operations. In the process, motorbus operations were encumbered with the work rules, craft structure, fare structure, tax levies, and service obligations of the electric street railway. Bus services that had been modestly profitable in loosely regulated "Mom and Pop" operations proved unprofitable when encumbered with the cost structure, service obligations, and uniform fare of street railway operations. Indeed, the extension of bus routes into sparsely settled territory and the acquisition of suburban bus operations served to further damage the financial position of street railways.[78] Access to capital became more problematic for all but a handful of very large properties, and the degradation of streetcar service through deferred maintenance and physical obsolescence continued as the industry norm.

As we have seen, efforts to recoup from the financial battering of the war years were frustrated by the selective loss of patronage, the increasing imbalance between peak and off-peak load factors, forced extension of streetcar service to outlying districts, and preemptive

TABLE 3-10 Patronage of Independent
and Street Railway-Affiliated
Bus Operations, 1920–1928
(in billions)

Year	Independent Bus Operations	Buses Operated by Street Railways
1920	200	204
1921	247	255
1922	401	419
1923	585	625
1924	758	850
1925	895	1,120
1926	840	1,365
1927	800	1,645
1928	749	1,740

Source: American Transit Association, *Transit Journal*, January 1936.

operation of suburban bus lines to preserve territorial monopoly and capture future traffic growth. Instead of recovery, the 1920s produced increasing financial distress.

The dilemma of even the most professionally managed and soundly capitalized operations is illustrated by the case of the Milwaukee Electric Railway and Light Company, a consolidated utility that was aggressively improving service to sustain its market share and investing capital to reduce operating costs. It reported the following discouraging results in 1927:

> The Milwaukee Electric Railway and Light Company operates a transportation system which thoroughly covers the City of Milwaukee and its suburban communities, besides reaching out to other cities to distances upwards of 100 miles.
>
> The communities served are all in a district where the number of automobiles has grown as rapidly as in any section of the United States. Moreover, the communities are all of that size in which there are no compelling reasons for effective restrictive measures concerning parking. Hence, owners of automobiles are free to utilize the same for business and pleasure without substantial restraint.
>
> The organized local transportation system serving this group of communities has, therefore, suffered its full share of positive loss in traffic, together with loss of opportunities for increased traffic with the growth of the population.
>
> As in many other communities similarly situated, the local public transportation problem has been further complicated by impaired load factor. It has required, for several years, more cars, more car station facilities, more power and more men, and of course greater investment to handle a stationary volume of traffic because the patronage has become more concentrated during the rush hour periods.
>
> Furthermore, the City of Milwaukee and its suburbs have experienced considerable expansion in area and building in the past few years. This has brought the problem of how to provide public transportation service to new and populous subdivisions growing up in the outskirts in all directions.
>
> Notwithstanding these disadvantages, the company has maintained a high standard of service to all of these communities during and since the war period.
>
> Through radical and original developments in power plant design and operation, power costs have been substantially reduced.
>
> It has increased the number of cars operated in Milwaukee city and suburban service by 145 or 27.7 per cent.
>
> By reconstruction of old equipment and reassembling into two-man trains, and through liberal introduction of one-man operated cars, it has increased maximum seats operated daily by 8,238 or 31.1 per cent.

Antique interurban railway equipment has been reconstructed into the highest speed and most luxurious type of rolling stock, supplemented by feeder lines of motor coaches, likewise of the speediest and most luxurious type.

The business of the interurban lines has been increased by rendering a high speed, regular, and efficient express service for the carriage of freight.

By means of the motor coach, the territory tributary to the interurban lines has been greatly expanded wherever there was a prospect that persistent operation of high class equipment on schedule would attract passenger business.

City and suburban local lines have been extended with rails where justified or as ordered by regulating authority, such extensions being further supplemented by cross-town motor bus lines and radial motor bus lines operating as a part of the railway system.

The local field had been thoroughly occupied by the company through early installation of motor buses wherever a reasonable demand or opportunity for the operation of such buses occurred. Certain lines of buses have been operated independently of railway service and at higher rates of fare where there were districts seeming to require such operation and desiring a class of service represented by a seat for every fare in high class equipment.[79]

Despite these aggressive steps to beat back the competition of the automobile and develop new markets, the property's general manager concluded that

The constantly increasing disadvantages of [unbalanced] load factor and traffic conditions generally [are] increasing the cost of service more rapidly than [can] be offset by improvements in devices or methods.

Such was the condition of one of the industry's premiere performers at the advent of the Great Depression. As Table 3-11 shows,

TABLE 3-11 Operating Ratio for Street Railways of Different Size, 1922 and 1927

Year	Industry-wide Average	Properties with Revenue in Excess of $1 Million	Properties with Revenue in Excess of $250,000 but Less than $1 Million	Properties with Revenues of Less than $250,000
1922	71.6%	70.7%	73.5%	81.2%
1927	74.9	72.8	85.5	95.0

Source: U.S. Bureau of the Census, *Electric Railways,* 1927 (Washington, D.C.: Government Printing Office, 1931).

the condition of most properties was even more tenuous, with the preponderance of companies teetering at the edge of bankruptcy. Thus, even before the depression, the transit industry's development had been arrested; its patronage was declining; its securities were held in low esteem; its credit was severely impaired; and its best efforts to stage a recovery and resume growth had proven counterproductive.

THE BUFFETING OF DEPRESSION AND WAR

The industrial depression of the 1930s led to the extinction of street railway operations in some 250 cities, accelerated the substitution of bus routes for streetcar lines, and precipitated disinvestment among transit properties large and small.[80] The loss of transit ridership that accompanied rising unemployment forced many properties into deficit operation, and even large operations found themselves in the widening circle of companies in acute financial distress.

While transit ridership had begun to decline several years before the depression, the coach miles of service operated had continued to increase in the late 1920s as street railways introduced motorbus service and extended their routes into suburban territories. As Table 3-12 shows, the trend toward increasing coach mileage flagged in the last year of full employment prior to the depression, a sharp decline in service followed as the economy faltered and joblessness soared. The depression halted the extension of bus service to outlying suburbs but hastened the adoption of buses for urban street operation.[81] As Table 3-12 shows, the coach miles of streetcar service declined much more rapidly than did the vehicle mileage of transit service per se, as bus routes were substituted for streetcar lines.

The substitution of buses for streetcars occurred for reasons that varied from property to property. In some cases, the substitution of bus for rail service afforded the only feasible strategy for eliminating the two-man crew used in streetcar operations. In other cases, streetcar displacement occurred when the physical deterioration of street rails precipitated a forced decision to replace trackage or find a more expedient way of sustaining operation. Many properties opted for bus substitution because they were unable to obtain the capital for track replacement, although it could have proved more economical than bus operation over the life cycle of the rail investment, given prevailing traffic densities and the state of development of bus technology.[82]

Table 3-13 shows a then contemporary assessment of the relative costs of replacing streetcar plant and equipment versus the substitution of bus service. As the table shows, there was a sizable differential in

TABLE 3-12 The Parallel Trends of Unemployment
and Transit Service, 1927–1940

Year	Nationwide Unemployment Rate (%)[1]	Vehicle Miles of Transit Service (millions)[2]	Coach Miles of Streetcar Service (millions)[2]
1927	3.3%	2,922	2,164
1928	4.2	3,002	2,113
1929	3.2	2,992	2,061
1930	8.7	2,930	1,995
1931	15.9	2,731	1,859
1932	23.6	2,439	1,690
1933	24.9	2,259	1,593
1934	21.7	2,312	1,586
1935	20.1	2,327	1,544
1936	16.9	2,433	1,543
1937	14.3	2,505	1,498
1938	19.9	2,434	1,380
1939	17.2	2,470	1,348
1940	14.6	2,596	1,316

[1] From U.S. Bureau of the Census, *Historical Statistics of the United States* (Washington, D.C.: Government Printing Office, 1976).
[2] From *Moody's Transportation Manual* (New York: Moody's Investor Service, Inc., 1982).

front-end capital costs that served as a serious obstacle to the replacement of streetcar plant and rolling stock.

Forced substitution became increasingly common during the depression because physical obsolescence plagued street railways by 1933 and the financial condition of most properties could be characterized as "unstable . . . and becoming increasingly acute."[83] Most properties were invading depreciation reserves to pay current expenses, and almost none was able to obtain outside capital to replace physically worn-out plant and equipment. Indeed, many properties were able to replace aging rolling stock and physically obsolete trackage only "through loans provided by stockholders endeavoring to avoid entire loss of their holdings through receivership or bond foreclosure."[84]

This is the context in which bus substitution decisions were typically reached. Relative to continued operation of *aging and obsolete* streetcar plant and equipment, bus substitution promised lower costs of maintenance and operation. Relative to the replacement of street railway rolling stock and trackage, the purchase of buses entailed a significantly lower capital expense. But bus operation typically entailed higher maintenance and operating costs than did the replace-

TABLE 3-13 Typical Financial Comparison of Modern Vehicles, 1940

	Surface Car	Trolley Bus	Gas Bus
Seating capacity	54	40	40
Round trip distance, miles	10.0	10.0	10.0
Hours of service per day; rush-nonrush	5-15	5-15	5-15
Headway, minutes	2.5-5.0	1.75-4.0	1.75-4.0
Average stops per mile	8-6	8-6	8-6
Duration of average stop, seconds	7-7	7-7	7-7
Round trip layover, minutes	4-5	4-5	4-5
Schedule speed, mph	13.6-15.6	13.6-15.6	12.5-14.5
Runtime excluding layover, minutes	45-39	45-39	48-42
Runtime including layover, minutes	49-44	49-44	52-47
Number of units required in service	20-9	28-11	30-12
Number of spares	2	3	5
Total number of units required	22	31	35
Annual mileage plus 3% deadhead	1,025,000	1,128,000	1,312,000
Annual hours plus 5% deadhead	80,000	140,100	112,500
Investment			
Cost of one vehicle	$ 15,000	$ 12,000	$ 11,000
Total cost of vehicles	330,000	372,000	385,000
Total cost of tracks	450,000		
Total cost of distribution system	50,000	45,000	
Total investment	830,000	417,000	385,000
Ratio of investment	216	108	100

Annual Charges

Maintenance of way and street, cents per vehicle mile	2.2	0.8	4.4
Maintenance of equipment	2.2	2.6	3.9
Power or fuel	4.6	3.1	7.7
Conducting transportation	7.5	7.4	
Traffic	0.1	0.1	0.1
General and miscellaneous	2.4	2.2	2.9
Depreciation of vehicles	1.8	3.0	4.7
Depreciation of way and street	1.8	0.2	
Taxes	0.8	0.5	2.4
Total annual charges, cents per vehicle mile	23.4	19.9	26.1
Ratio	90	76	100
Total annual charges, cents per seat mile	0.43	0.50	0.66
Ratio	65	76	100
Total annual charges	$239,800	$224,500	$342,400
Ratio of annual charges	70	66	100

Source: Francis R. Thompson, *Electric Transportation* (Scranton, Penn.: International Textbook Company, 1940).

ment of streetcar track and rolling stock. Unable to finance the alternative that would have minimized long-run costs, many street railways sought to minimize short-term obligations as their only feasible strategy for weathering the depression.[85] Thus, bus substitution represented a calculated decision to shoulder higher long-run operating costs as the unavoidable penalty for sustaining operation until both the economy and traffic recovered. Also favoring bus substitution were municipal street paving changes that were assessed against streetcar lines but not bus operations.

As a consequence, bus substitution occurred on some routes with traffic densities more appropriate for streetcar operation, and the depression-era reduction of peak-hour capacity actually overshot the decline of ridership.

Properties planning bus substitution in the early years of the depression could consider two rubber-tired technologies: the gasoline-powered motorbus and the electric trolleybus. Both technologies permitted curb loading, but as Table 3-13 showed, the electric trolleybus could afford service more economically than could the motorbus on routes with medium- to high-density traffic and pronounced peaking. On the downside of the ledger, the trolleybus required a larger initial investment, was more susceptible to system failure, and could not be rerouted in the instance of either a short-term emergency or a long-term shift in the spatial pattern of transit traffic.[86]

By 1939, the development of a mature diesel engine afforded transit properties a third choice—an oil-burning motorbus more reliable, more fuel efficient, and less maintenance intensive than gasoline-powered models. The primary manufacturer of diesel-powered units was General Motors, and its strategy for marketing diesel coaches has proved a source of enormous controversy.

In 1937, only 62 diesel coaches were owned and operated by U.S. transit properties, and most street railways were understandably reluctant to adopt a technology that was viewed as essentially unproven in sustained urban operation.[87] This posed a no-win situation for diesel bus manufacturers—General Motors, Mack, and Twin Coach. Diesel units would not sell until experience data justifying acquisition were available; but experience data could not be assembled in the absence of sales and operation. To break this logjam, General Motors joined with an oil and rubber company to capitalize a transit management organization with the financing necessary to acquire failing streetcar systems and reequip them with diesel buses.

The holding company thus formed—National City Lines—eventually acquired some 100 distressed street railways and converted them to diesel bus operation.[88] By 1940, 75 U.S. transit companies were operating 680 diesel buses, primarily of General Motors manufac-

ture, a dramatic increase over the 62 coaches in operation when
National City Lines began its acquisition campaign.[89]

The National City Lines Controversy

The acquisition of streetcar lines and their conversion to diesel
motorbuses has been characterized as an insidious industrial conspiracy
designed to destroy mass transit and stimulate the sale of automobiles.[90] It can more accurately be characterized as corporate strategy to
sell diesel buses by creating first a pilot market and later a sole-source
supplier relationship with effectively captive consumers. Its most important consequence was not the displacement of streetcar systems—
the exigencies of the depression were already forcing conversion to bus
operation long before the formation of National City Lines. Rather,
the lasting consequence of National City Lines' entry into the transit
business was the dominance of a single manufacturer in the diesel bus
market and the preemption of routes and markets that might have been
more economically served by the electric trolleybus. Properties that
planned conversion to a mixed trolley and motorbus fleet with each
technology matched to its appropriate field of operation abandoned
such conversion plans after acquisition by National City Lines.[91] As a
result, the technological development of the trolleybus languished in
the United States, while the diesel bus emerged as the industry's predominant vehicle technology. At the same time, General Motors
emerged as the predominant manufacturer of the diesel vehicle.

Is this a matter of important consequence? Our best judgment is
"probably yes." General Motors' preemption of the bus market served
to dampen competition in transit coach manufacturing and thus
probably retarded innovations in both diesel and electric bus design
that might have reduced transit operating costs. In the absence of
significant competitive incentive, few improvements in diesel bus technology were made after the 1950s, although improvements of European
origin establish that the potential for advancement was not yet exhausted. Limited competition in the manufacturing sector may also
have permitted oligopolistic pricing of diesel coaches and parts, but to
what extent is unknown. We do know that the virtual demise of trolleybus manufacturing in the 1960s imposed inflated costs on properties
that adopted that technology in the 1930s and 1940s.[92]

Probably as important, the preemption of the trolleybus market
by diesel buses left most properties operating a vehicle notorious for its
noise, rumble, and fumes. While the diesel bus may have served its
users well, it was generally held in low esteem by nonusers: motorists,
pedestrians, cyclists, and the residents of homes abutting bus routes.
Thus, it seems not too unlikely that the diesel bus served the transit

industry poorly in terms of public image and public relations. Indeed, transit would be perceived more as a nuisance than an asset in the 1950s, undoubtedly retarding the transition to public ownership and operation.

The National City Lines venture was, in short, a market-breaching and market-cornering strategy rather than an elaborate conspiracy to destroy the last competitive threat to the automobile. Its importance lies in the concentration of economic advantage in the bus manufacturing industry rather than in the supposed destruction of "viable" street railways. In any case, other developments that occurred during the depression years were more important for the future of the transit industry than was any role played by National City Lines. Unfortunately, all too many students of urban affairs have neglected these more important developments in the process of debating the conspiracy theory of transit's decline. As we shall see, the programmatic content of the New Deal and the changes it wrought in the way the nation planned and financed urban highway development was matter of far greater consequence to mass transit in the postwar era.

State and Federal Involvement in Urban Road Building

Prior to the depression, state and federal spending for road and highway development was limited to rural construction, whereas urban road building was a city and county responsibility, primarily financed with property taxes. As the depression battered local economies, taxpayers were forced to default on property tax payments, and local tax collections declined precipitously, eroding the financial position of local governments.[93] Declining property tax collections curtailed municipal road-building activity and generated intense political pressure to revise statutes that prevented the use of state highway funds within city boundaries. Urban representatives in state legislatures organized to rewrite the statutory formulas apportioning state highway funds, adding revenue-sharing provisions sought by city and county governments. At the national level, the Roosevelt administration sought and obtained legislation permitting the expenditure of federal highway funds in urban areas. Indeed, federal involvement in metropolitan road building was initially motivated by macroeconomic concerns—the felt need to generate public works employment for those on the urban relief rolls.[94] The resulting changes in state and federal statutes permitted intergovernmental transfers to fill the road-building void created by the collapse of urban property tax collections.

Federal and state spending for urban roads was a significant development, not only because it accelerated highway construction but also because it brought with it a fundamental change in the locus of institutional responsibility for urban road planning. Consistent with the traditions of the federal government's rural highway program, Congress lodged the responsibility for spending urban highway subventions with state highway departments rather than local planning or engineering officials. State highway departments first assumed a lead agency role in urban road development with the passage of the Emergency Relief and Construction Act of 1932—an emergency appropriations measure designed to create temporary jobs in the construction of public works. This emergency arrangement was broadened by the Hayden-Cartwright Act of 1934, which permitted the expenditure of routine federal aid subventions in urban areas. Federal participation in urban road building was made permanent and was institutionalized with the passage of the Federal Aid Highway Act of 1944. The 1944 act authorized the states to spend federal highway funds on the urban extensions of state primary highways and instructed the Bureau of Public Roads to designate a national system of interstate highways, also eligible for federal aid.[95]

The 1944 Act—a landmark event in the evolution of U.S. highway policy—equipped state highway departments with the financial wherewithal to play a dominant role in urban highway development on a permanent basis. In combination with 1943 legislation permitting state highway departments to use federal funds for right-of-way acquisition, the 1944 Act positioned state highway departments to assume a lead role in postwar highway planning and development in metropolitan areas. While the act did not abridge the powers of cities and counties to construct roads or manage traffic, its consequence was a *de facto* shift in the locus of institutional responsibility for urban transportation development as a new and dominant fiscal partner entered the urban arena on a permanent basis.

State highway departments brought to urban areas a design and planning doctrine based on years of experience building rural highways. They also brought to cities the financial wherewithal to acquire new rights of way and construct highway facilities of unprecedented scale and scope—facilities we now know as freeways. The urban freeway concept emerged from the convergence of rural highway experience, state design doctrine, and the financial leverage afforded by state highway accounts augmented by federal aid. The facilities planned and engineered by state highway departments would be fundamentally different in concept, function, and scale from the boulevards, parkways, and expressways planned for postwar development by municipal planning and engineering departments.

To understand the emergence of the freeway concept, we must examine the formative years of state highway doctrine as it was developed and articulated in the context of rural engineering experience.

As we shall see, the freeway is more a rural import than an evolutionary upscaling of urban boulevards or parkways. State freeways would present a significantly different competitive challenge to mass transit than that afforded by facilities built to parkway or boulevard scale.

The Origins of State Highway Policy

At the close of the horsepower era, rural road construction was typically a responsibility of county governments. County road philosophy emphasized the construction of roads on alignments determined by property and section lines—a virtual guarantee of circuitous routing as the traveled way bent and turned with fence and property lines. Nevertheless, it was accepted practice that the right-of-way should be subordinated to the rights of property, and circuitous routing was the norm in agricultural districts.[96] Such roads offered less than satisfactory service for long-distance travel and primarily served a farm-to-railhead function. By the 1920s, the power and speed of automobiles had significantly outdistanced the design concept of county-built roads. The sharp curves, restricted sight distances, narrow widths, and undulating profiles of roads built in the horsedrawn era posed a serious hazard when traveled by vehicles capable of sustained speed in excess of 40 miles per hour.[97]

Beginning in the 1890s, state road departments were formed to build more serviceable intercity routes—roads to connect county seats and urban centers. Early in the development of state road systems, engineering professionals articulated a new alignment and construction philosophy that emphasized direct routing, the taking of right-of-way, and building for permanence. Limited financial resources constrained the implementation of this "scientific road-building" philosophy in many states, but it represented the engineering optimum toward which state highway departments strove. The earliest state highways—built on rights-of-way acquired or ceded by county governments—were of lesser design and were rapidly obsoleted by the growth of motoring and the increasing mechanical sophistication of automobile engines.

As accidents mounted, state highway departments obtained powers to condemn property and build on new alignments, and the leading states pioneered in the articulation of geometric design standards. Using geometric principles, states scaled up their design standards to afford the sweeping curves, unrestricted sightlines, wide lanes, serviceable shoulders, smooth pavements, and gently sloping grades necessary for high-speed motoring. They also adopted the principle of uniform design—the philosophy that a highway should afford a uniform level of performance from terminus to terminus so that accidents are not occasioned by a sudden and unexpected change in driving regime.

Despite these advances in road design, accidents continued to increase with increasing speeds and the growth of traffic. Many of these accidents could be attributed to cross traffic, turning movements, and differential speeds at the margin of urban settlements or in the rural towns through which state highways passed.[98] Traffic interference and accidents attributable to cross traffic and turning movements led to the concept of a limited-access facility, sequestered by excess right-of-way from abutting property and local traffic movements. The design objective of limited access facilities was to quarantine high-speed traffic, separate through and local movements, minimize cross traffic, and prevent the degradation of highway performance attributable to the development of roadside property. Thus, limiting access served to minimize traffic interference and protect highway investments from the premature obsolescence associated with encroachment by roadside development.

The premature obsolescence of the facilities first built by state highway departments—their obsolescence due to increasing speed, increasing traffic volume, and encroaching uses—was an important dimension of the rural highway experience. Obsolescence was an embarrassment and an anathema by the 1930s, a mistake of past engineering to be avoided by future planning.[99] The result was another upscaling of state standards: facilities would be sized to serve future traffic and designed to accommodate future speeds with a sizable margin of tolerance for prediction error.

These elements of the rural experience—the object lesson of premature obsolescence and the engineering response of geometric design and limited access—provided the intellectual foundation for urban freeway planning. Urban freeways are a concatenation of rural design standards—facilities engineered to accommodate speeds encountered in interregional travel and sized to avoid the engineering embarrassment of premature obsolescence.

The urban freeways that would be built in the postwar period were a creature of the rural experience of state highway departments, but they were also a product of the apparatus created to finance highways. By the late 1930s, most states had adopted gasoline taxes and motor vehicle registration fees as their primary method of financing highway development. The gas tax and registration fee are imposts that place the financial burden of highway construction on highway users. In this sense, they are a fair, equitable, and relatively popular form of taxation that commensurates burdens and benefits. They are not, however, a *use* tax that achieves a perfect correspondence between taxes paid and value received. They are an administratively efficient proxy for use charges, but a loose proxy at best. They fail as a true proxy because the user-tax/revenue-apportionment apparatus permits sizable cross-subsidies between different classes of highway users and between different geographic areas. It is well established, for example, that urban motorists cross-subsidized the highway usage of intercity trucking until truck imposts were increased in 1982.[100] Less frequently discussed is the sizable cross-subsidy received by peak-hour motorists from taxes paid by off-peak users.

The co-mingling of tax revenues derived from autos and trucks, from peak and off-peak users, and from urban, suburban, and rural highway usage, is universally characteristic of state highway accounts. Co-mingling permitted cross-subsidy, in turn, permitting states to shoulder the financial burden of urban freeways that were sized and scoped to serve future volumes of peak-hour traffic. Highway facilities scaled to future volumes of peak-hour traffic were beyond the financial reach of the city and county jurisdictions that dominated urban road-building until 1944. But the wealthier states could dodge the financial constraint encountered by local transportation officials and could build facilities at freeway scale because revenue co-mingling and *intertemporal* cross-subsidy permitted them to do so. Thus, in the financial sense particularly, the urban freeway was something very different from an evolutionary upscaling of urban boulevards and parkways. Freeways are a creature of state and federal fuel taxes, not city property taxes.

With the passage of the 1944 Federal Aid Highway Act, the wealthier urban states were equipped with the financial wherewithal to augment state user imposts and execute freeway plans based on their accumulated rural experience. Those plans would embody geometric design, high-speed performance, and excess right-of-way acquisition.

As World War II drew to a close and Congress began considering postwar legislation, President Roosevelt exhorted public officials at every level of government to prepare a "ready shelf" of plans for postwar construction projects. A massive public works program was needed, Roosevelt argued, to buffer the transition from wartime to peacetime employment and take up industrial slack.

Governments at every level responded, framing plans for road and highway construction. It is informative to compare the urban highway plans prepared by municipal authorities with those prepared by the highway departments of leading states. Cities typically prepared plans based on a mix of traffic management strategies:

Parkways and expressways to carry long-distance through traffic and quarantine the movements of heavy trucks

Improved mass transit to provide downtown access and afford peak-hour capacity

Boulevard widenings and traffic engineering to manage the flow of local traffic

The parkways and expressways proposed in these plans were modestly scaled facilities; they were to be built at a scale consistent with restrained speeds of 40 miles per hour and minimal land acquisition requirements. Because modestly scaled, low-speed facilities were planned, existing alignments and right-of-way would be used with additions at the margin. Only partial access control was contemplated, and the sweeping curves and elaborate interchanges typical of full freeway design were not proposed by city officials attentive to the cost and controversy of right-of-way acquisition.[101]

The expressways proposed by city officials were to serve a quarantine function—separating long- and short-distance traffic and insulating cities from the intrusion of heavy trucks and through traffic. The peak-period capacity requirements of commuters were to be met by mass transit, whereas expressways were to serve a different function, that of insulating the complex and sometimes fragile social functions of local roadspace from the impacts of through traffic.

The traffic management plans developed by city planners and traffic engineers were only partially implemented as city officials opted to conserve municipal revenues and cede primary responsibility for large-scale investment to state highway departments. State highway investments were not forced or thrust upon cities as some recent commentaries would suggest. They were actively and aggressively sought by cities seeking to capture the largest possible share of state funds and preserve local revenues for other purposes. Indeed, the legislative and political challenge perceived by urban officials was to overcome the long-established rural bias of state spending for highways. Defending municipal prerogatives from state encroachment was not an issue, nor would it become one for years to come.

For the sake of continuity, we will discuss the impacts of postwar freeway development on mass transit before returning to complete our discussion of the depression and war years.

To understand the impact of urban freeways on mass transit, it is essential to recognize that freeways represented only a relatively small increment in urban roadspace and urban highway capacity, but added significantly to the urban territory within the reach of a 30- or 40-minute trip. It is also essential to recognize that a freeway is a trunk-line facility that serves to attract, focus, and concentrate traffic movements because of the speed advantage it affords over travel on surface routes.[102]

By increasing the speed and reach of both truck and auto travel, freeways changed the geography of locational advantage in metropolitan areas. By focusing and concentrating traffic movements, freeways delivered traffic to central business districts in volumes that would overwhelm surface street systems and confound the operation and scheduling of mass transit. The traffic conflict and changes in locational advantage that freeways produced were probably of greater consequence to mass transit than was the direct competition afforded by these new facilities. *Direct* competition between transit systems and freeways systems was most important in those few cities where radial freeways offered service parallel to that afforded by rapid transit or a commuter railroad. In these centers, the development of radial freeways prevented rapid transit systems and commuter railroads from pricing their service so as to reflect faithfully the distance traveled and the true cost of peak-hour service. As off-peak patronage declined in the post-war period, these systems could not resort to true peak-hour, distance-based pricing as a strategy of financial recovery, because no toll or charge was levied for the use of peak-hour roadspace.[103]

In most cities, direct competition between the freeway system and the transit system was restricted to a relatively small slice of the commuter market. Transit systems served trip makers in the short-haul and medium-haul market; freeways served medium- and long-distance trip makers. Thus, direct competition occurred only in the medium-haul market entered reluctantly or preemptively by street railways in the 1920s. Already the least remunerative of transit markets, the continued operation of the suburban extensions of central-city transit systems became increasingly burdensome as their patrons abandoned transit in favor of freeway travel.

To recoup losses on suburban service, transit properties sought repeated fare increases in the late 1940s and the 1950s. In terms of the value of the service received, the uniform fare increases obtained during this period fell most heavily on short-haul riders. Increases in the flat fare served to accentuate already burdensome cross-subsidies between transit's central-city and suburban riders. At the same time, the automobile traffic delivered by freeways to central districts impeded transit operations and attenuated the headways that could be maintained with a fleet of constant size.[104] Fare increases and congestion-attenuated headways served to erode transit's primary market: short-haul ridership. Where parking availability permitted, these riders abandoned transit in favor of the automobile and local street system. The destruction of the short-haul market through service attenuation and misguided pricing explains why transit was unable to contract to a stable base of operations in the market niche for which it is best suited.

It is important to emphasize that the destruction of the short-haul market was not a result of direct competition between freeways and transit systems. It was, instead, an indirect consequence of competition in the already tenuous medium-haul market and a product of the central business district traffic conflict that resulted from the concentrated traffic volumes delivered by radial freeways. This dynamic was compounded by regulatory decisions that amounted to a mandate to maintain service in suburban markets by increasing cross-subsidies between long- and short-haul riders.

Changes in the geography of locational advantage that accompanied urban freeway construction also damaged transit systems by accelerating the loss of ridership. Indeed, many observers of transit's decline have argued that the sprawling pattern of development fostered by mortgage assistance and freeway construction is the causal nexus of the industry's postwar financial distress.

There is little substance to this argument unless "sprawl" is understood as simple but misleading shorthand for complex changes in the organization of urban activities that occurred in the postwar period. Transit *was* disadvantaged by the migration of middle-income households and by the relocation and reorganization of industry and retailing that began in the 1920s and accelerated after World War II;[105] it was *not* disadvantaged by sprawl per se. The developmental densities that characterized postwar suburbs—sprawl, for short—did little more than foreclose further unwise service expansion of the sort that occurred in the 1920s. At least, that would be the case until the availability of federal and state subsidies for transit-generated political pressure from outlying suburbs for a "fair share" of the service financed with tax support.[106]

Transit's financial base *was* damaged by changes in urban activity patterns that accompanied the relocation of households and the reorganization of economic activity. These changes were intimately related to the co-development of freeways and trucking and the coordinate growth of the suburbs and auto ownership. The co-development of freeways and trucking freed light industry from the need to locate on railroad lines, allowing manufacturing plants to relocate on less costly suburban land and realize reorganization economies associated with new plant layouts. Relocation, of course, diminished transit ridership in the central city.

More important still were changes in the location and organization of activities that depressed off-peak ridership. The postwar development of the urban supermarket is one such case. The supermarket is a product of home refrigeration, the trunkspace of the automobile, refrigerated trucking, and a logistics system made possible by freeway development. Supermarkets fundamentally changed the shopping behavior of urban residents. In the process, the grocery, the butcher, the bakery, and the variety store that had served the transit rider with a twine-handled bag were gradually displaced from the urban scene. For transit, the loss of ridership was important because most occurred during the off-peak hours.

Decisions of middle-income households to relocate in the suburbs had a similarly depressant effect on off-peak ridership. As the middle class left the central city, so did the buying power necessary to maintain downtown retailing in a position of metropolitan preeminence. That preeminence was lost as retailers located shopping centers near their prime customers. Off-peak and weekend transit ridership was lost, in turn, as the attraction of shopping downtown declined—and with it the quality and selection of merchandise to be found there. A similar story could be told about downtown entertainment districts—their decline and the corresponding loss of evening ridership by transit systems.

As this discussion suggests, the speed of travel and locational flexibility freeways permitted was an intimate part of a complex process of relocation and reorganization that transformed urban activity patterns in the postwar period. Changes in the geographic and temporal pattern of travel that accompanied relocation and reorganization would deprive transit of the traffic density and traffic balance needed to sustain profitability. It was the *loss of traffic density and balance in established transit markets, not development at low residential density, that damaged transit in the postwar years.*

Other Developments During the Depression and War Years

As we have seen, the exigencies of the depression involved the federal government in urban road finance. Federal spending brought with it state administrative control of metropolitan highway development, which in turn produced a significant change in urban engineering philosophy and highway design scale. Other legislative initiatives of the Roosevelt administration would further damage the financial position of transit properties, also without intent. The most important of these was the Fair Labor Standards Act of 1938, which established the eight-hour workday and five-day workweek as a national standard for hourly workers. The five-day workweek was embraced by the Roosevelt administration as a strategy to create jobs by dividing the available hours of work among a large number of workers.[107] Prior to the depression, six-day workweeks were the norm in the manufacturing sector and the number of hours worked daily varied significantly from industry to industry.

The standardization of the workday and workweek had two effects on mass transit: it sharply reduced Saturday patronage and it accentuated the peaking experienced during the weekday rush hours. Peaking increased because firms opted for a common eight-to-five schedule as their response to the eight-hour workday.

The effects of the Fair Labor Standards Act were not felt by transit properties until the postwar period. This lag is attributable to the curtailed hours of work available during the depression and the emergency production schedules of the war period. With the return to postwar economic normalcy, the lagged adoption of the five-day work-week may have reduced transit patronage by as much as 10 to 15 percent. The loss of Saturday work-trip ridership was more punishing for rail than for bus systems because these properties required heavier traffic volumes and larger cash flows to amortize their capital investment. Thus, the five-day workweek gave further impetus to the conversion from rail to bus operation that accelerated in the postwar period.

The conversion from rail to bus was given further impetus by antitrust legislation directed against public utility holding companies. The Public Utilities Holding Company Act of 1935 required utility trusts to divest captive holdings including electric street railways.[108] This damaged those street railways that had obtained electricity at privileged rates or had used the credit of the parent organization to borrow at favorable interest rates. In other cases, forced divestment provided a convenient excuse to end a corporate marriage that had gone sour long before. In any case, the divorce of street railways and electric utilities accelerated the abandonment of rail operations and the conversion to bus service.

The conversion process was stayed temporally by World War II. During the war years, transit patronage recovered dramatically, exceeding its previous peak recorded in 1927. The wartime ridership peak was attributable to both economic recovery and wartime conservation measures—gas and tire rationing, a national highway speed limit of 35 miles per hour, and the cessation of automobile production. Ridership peaked in 1946 under the influence of billeted travel by servicemen and continuing shortages of gasoline, tires, and auto parts.

While patronage recovered from its depression slump and the industry's operating ratio improved mildly, the war years were no blessing for mass transit. Pressed into overtime service throughout the war, transit plant and equipment had reached an advanced state of physical and mechanical fatigue by 1946. Extended hours of operation and deferred maintenance led to significant deterioration of both rail and rolling stock—literally exhausting the industry's physical assets by war's end. Precipitous disinvestment and conversion to bus operation would follow as the street railway's contribution to the industry's output shrunk from 40 percent in 1940 to 35 percent in 1946 and 11 percent in 1954.[109]

Wartime inflation—consumer prices rose 33 percent from 1941 to 1946—also proved damaging to transit although its impacts would not be felt until after the war. Fares were held virtually constant during the war years, and transit labor exercised considerable restraint in wartime bargaining.[110] Due to wage restraint and the dramatic increase in wartime ridership, the industry's aggregate net revenues increased some 38 percent from 1940 to 1946 in real dollar terms.[111] During the same period, the real wages of transit workers actually declined as wage adjustments lagged inflation. This built pressure for catch-up wage increases and would lead to an unparalleled number of strikes and work stoppages in the postwar period. As important, the settlements eventually agreed to in the first years following World War II would require an increase of almost 50 percent in the average fare by 1950, or a 35 percent fare increase in real dollar terms.[112] These fare increases would combine with the return to economic normalcy, the restoration of gasoline supplies, the renewed production of motor vehicles, and the acceleration of urban highway construction to produce precipitous loss of transit ridership in the postwar period. Moreover, it would be a managerially and physically exhausted industry that would have to face the monumental financial difficulties to be encountered in that period.

THE ERA OF PRECIPITOUS DECLINE

From its 1946 peak, nationwide transit ridership declined 26 percent by 1950 and another 28 percent in the succeeding four years. Table 3-14 shows the trend of patronage from 1946 to 1974 in four-year increments, a 28-year period in which the U.S. transit industry lost 70 percent of the ridership it reported in 1946. The most precipitous loss of ridership occurred in the first years of the postwar period—*before* the freeway construction boom that followed the creation of the

TABLE 3-14 The Trend of Transit Ridership, 1946–1974

Four-Year Increment	Percentage Change in Ridership
1946–1950	−26.2%
1950–1954	−28.1
1954–1958	−21.5
1958–1962	−10.7
1962–1966	−7.0
1966–1970	−9.3
1970–1974	−5.4

Source: American Transit Association and American Public Transit Association estimates as reported in *Moody's Transportation Manual* (New York: Moody's Investors Service, Inc., 1981).

federal highway trust fund in 1956 and *before* congressional authorization of accelerated spending for the interstate highway system at a 90:10 federal-state matching ratio. Transit's most precipitous decline thus occurred during the relatively sluggish start-up phase of urban freeway development, and the rapidity of that decline cannot be attributed in any large measure to federal and state spending for freeway and expressway construction.

To explain the loss of ridership that occurred in the postwar period, it is essential to understand the workings of three different dynamics. We can characterize the first of these as normalization—the downward normalization or "correction" of ridership that occurred with the end of gas and tire rationing, the return to "normal" peacetime employment levels, and the lagged introduction of the five-day workweek. The second dynamic is supply-side in character. Postwar wage increases combined with declining ridership to increase transit operating costs and depress passenger revenues.[113] Responding to an increasingly acute financial squeeze, properties sought to increase fares and reduce costs—the latter by shedding service. Fare increases and service reduction discouraged ridership—particularly among short-distance riders.

The third dynamic depressing transit ridership was the growth of personal income and automobile ownership and the consequent reorganization of urban activities to serve an increasingly "auto-mobile" population.[114] Transit's gradual secular decline is associated with the second and third dynamics, while the particularly precipitous loss of ridership in the immediate postwar period was the product of normalization and emergency fare increases precipitated by catch-up wage settlements negotiated during the war years. Thus, transit's postwar decline involved both an element of one-time correction and an element of secular competitive erosion.

The competitive erosion experienced in the postwar period was different from that of the 1920s in one very significant regard. During the late 1920s, transit properties in the largest cities generally held their own, and the ridership of commuter railroads and rapid transit systems actually increased. In the late 1940s and in the 1950s, large-city systems joined the ranks of properties with declining ridership and declining net revenues.

The difference in the fortunes of rail operations in the 1920s and the 1950s is attributable to intrametropolitan shifts in the geography of household location and retail activity. These shifts occurred because the postwar economy permitted an increasing percentage of American households to afford home and auto ownership and the move to the suburbs. The exodus of middle-income households from the central city was paralleled by a shift in the locus of retail and recreation activity.[115] Suburban malls and main streets boomed while downtown declined from its preeminent position as a mecca for shopping and entertainment, producing consequent change in the geography of urban travel. As a result, the radial geometry of rail systems became increasingly dissonant with the geography of off-peak travel. Stated another way, rising incomes changed the spatial pattern of urban travel, compounding the imbalance of peak and off-peak transit ridership.[116] The economic consequences of an increasingly unbalanced traffic base are evident from an Interstate Commerce Commission (ICC) investigation of the financial problems of railroad commuter services. We will quote the ICC's findings at some length because they effectively illustrate the particular dilemma associated with selective and unbalanced loss of patronage:

> The causes of the increasing unprofitability of commutation service are essentially the same as those affecting passenger traffic generally, namely a decrease in business and an increase in operating expenses, which because of the adverse conditions peculiar to this service are abnormally high.
>
> The increase in motor travel between cities and their suburbs is of course the principal but not the sole reason for the decline in commutation traffic. The widespread adoption of the five-day week has made Saturday a non-business day along with Sunday. The decentralization of retail business with the commercial growth of the suburbs has lessened the demand for off-peak train service by housewives on shopping trips to the city. Night trains for suburbanites seeking amusement in the city have become unnecessary because of television, so it is said.
>
> For the most part, therefore, the commutation traffic is concentrated in two morning hours and two evening hours 5 days a week. For example, at New York City the New York Central requires 304 coaches in handling its rush-hour traffic and 263 coaches for the evening traffic which extends over a somewhat longer period. For its off-peak period 70 coaches are sufficient. Hence this carrier is able to use its entire commutation fleet for only about 15 percent of the time and only 20 percent of its equipment during the remaining 85 percent. During the idle period the cars not only earn no revenue but must be stored on tracks in metropolitan areas which are expensive to own and maintain.
>
> The concentration of traffic also has the effect of requiring the railroads to pay compensation to their engine and train employees engaged in this service during periods of the day when they are necessarily off duty. A round-trip in a morning commutation run usually requires only a few hours, but since a crew is entitled to a minimum of 8 hours pay, it is usually called on for service also in the afternoon or evening. This service commonly terminates some 10 or 12 hours after the time of starting work in the morning, and the total period is called the "spread of assignment."

The engine and train employees in commutation service are paid according to a special rule for what is known as short turnaround passenger service, "no single trip of which exceeds 80 miles, including suburban and branch-line service." There are basic day's wages for these employees, based on an 8-hour day, but overtime, which is very important for reasons before indicated, is computed according to what is familiarly known as the "8 within 9 hour overtime rule." This rule in substance requires that all time within the spread of assignment form first report to final release must be paid for at the regular hourly rate, unless within the first 9 hours there is a period of continuous release in excess of one hour. In that event one hour may be deducted from total time paid for. If the release period of more than one hour extends beyond the 9-hour limit, only the period within the first 9 hours may be deducted. Release periods of one hour or less are paid for in all cases.

The effect of this rule is illustrated by the following actual example: an assistant conductor reports for duty at a New York Central suburban station at 5:14 A.M. for a run to New York City and is released from duty at 8:03 A.M. with nothing to do thereafter until 4:10 P.M. when he reports for work on an afternoon run to the same suburban station, where he is released from duty at 7:50 P.M. The spread of assignment is 14 hours and 36 minutes, involving 6 hours and 29 minutes of time actually worked and 8 hours and 7 minutes of uninterrupted release time in the middle of the day. Under the present rules the compensation for this service consists of one basic day's pay and 5 hours and 36 minutes of overtime.

Another example pertains to ticket collectors on suburban trains of the Pennsylvania to and from Philadelphia, who in the summer of 1956 had an average daily spread of assignment of 9 hours and 40 minutes. The average time actually worked was 6 hours and 40 minutes. Their average time paid for but not worked was 23 hours and 22 minutes and their average earnings per day were $17.92, based on a basic daily wage rate of $15.15. However, their compensation was also subject to a monthly guarantee rule providing for payment of $454.50 per month (30 times basic daily rate of $15.15) regardless of the number of days worked per month, paid also without regard to the amount of overtime earned during the month.[117]

As the ICC's inquiry found, the selective loss of off-peak ridership presented a dilemma for commuter railroads—as it did for other transit properties. This is because the industry's work rules, craft structure, pay schedules, and fare structure were developed in the era when public conveyance was the dominant form of urban transportation. The fare structure and labor contracts fashioned in the early 1900s suited the pattern of traffic that prevailed before the diffusion of the automobile when Saturday, Sunday, and evening ridership made a major contribution to the patronage base of public transportation. The traffic balance and traffic density necessary for profitable operation began to unravel in the 1920s and was destroyed in the postwar period. Forced service contraction and a succession of fare increases followed, depressing ridership further but extending the financial staying power of the larger urban properties. Indeed, the staying power of this depressed industry is nothing short of remarkable, considering the duration of its economic distress. The industry's staying power can be explained, in part, by its developmental history. The street railways assembled in the 1890s and early 1900s were loose amalgamations of horsecar routes, never fully rationalized in the process of consolidation. In Philadelphia, for instance, the traction company was an amalgamation of 57 independent horsecar operations.[118] As the American Electric Railway Association would comment,

> For the most part, present street railway systems consist merely of a grouping of former separate lines built with little regard to a community plan or to the future. . . . In many instances the lines thus joined together afforded only circuitous and indirect routes for a communitywide transportation service. . . . In other instances there was unnecessary duplicate trackage [and overlapping routes]. . . . A relatively large amount of relocation, rerouting and abandonment of unnecessary trackage was needed to mold these assembled lines into efficient community-wide systems. At this critical point, street railways were suddenly plunged into acute financial difficulty [by the onset of industrial depression].[119]

The redundancy and duplication of service still evident by the late 1940s and early 1950s afforded transit systems significant opportunities to achieve operating economies by pruning and rationalizing service. The shedding of costs associated with redundant routes and now poorly patronized nighttime service prolonged the economic life of transit systems in the postwar years as did the fare increases obtained in this period. Sustained operation was achieved, however, at a high price in terms of lost ridership and declining contribution to the host city's economic well-being. Nonetheless, service contraction and fare increases provided a strategy for warding off foreclosure and prolonging solvency.

Conversion from streetcar to bus service served as a complement to network rationalization efforts. It permitted the rerouting and reallocation of service and the replacement of war-worn equipment without burdening transit properties with the excessive debt obligations that would have been involved in replacing streetcar plant and equipment. Perhaps as important, bus conversion afforded a politically pragmatic strategy for shedding the obligation to provide frequent service in districts where streetcar operation had become unrenumerative because of changes in the pattern of travel or the loss of resident population.

During the 1950s, transit companies found ways to shed costs and rationalize service that were sufficient to sustain operation, but not to increase profitability or restore financial stability. Thus, by the late 1950s, an increasing number of properties were willing to explore public acquisition as last-resort strategy for salvaging some value from past investment.[120]

Public Ownership

The earliest major initiatives in the direction of public ownership occurred in New York and Boston where municipal government financed rapid transit systems in the 1890s but leased them to private companies for operation. The first voter approval of operation in public ownership occurred in Chicago, but public acquisition was never consummated due to protracted litigation. Actual public ownership and operation was first effectuated in San Francisco in 1909 and then in Seattle two years later.[121] After Detroit purchased its street railway in 1922, municipal acquisition activity waned until 1940, when New York City purchased the city's major private subway and surface properties. Cleveland followed in 1942. By war's end, only five major properties were publicly owned, but they accounted for close to 20 percent of the nation's transit ridership. Another wave of public acquisitions began in the postwar years, triggered by the specter of financial collapse. The Chicago Transit Authority was formed in 1947 to acquire private transit properties in that city, and public ownership was effectuated in Los Angeles, Oakland, and Sacramento, California, in the 1950s.[122] By 1955, properties in public ownership accounted for approximately 35 percent of the industry's ridership and almost half by 1960.[123]

Public acquisition was primarily a big-city phenomenon through the 1950s. Private operations in the smaller cities typically were allowed to fade into extinction through service contraction and business failure. As Table 3-15 shows, cities with a population of less than 500,000 accounted for half of the nation's transit ridership in 1945 but less than 30 percent by 1970.

Public acquisition warded off bond foreclosures that would have led to the extinction of service and the sale of marketable assets, but it did not bring economic recovery. Fare increases and service contraction continued under public ownership, as public authorities continued to manage transit operations on a cost-recovery basis.

Economic stability proved elusive, in part, because of steady and successful pressure from transit labor to increase base wages. Pressure to increase wages was particularly intense in the postwar period because of the wage restraint exercised by transit unions during World War II.[124]

TABLE 3-15 Proportion of Total
Transit Ridership Occurring
in Cities of Less than 500,000 Population,
Selected Years, 1945–1970

Year	Smaller City Ridership Share:
1945	49.8%
1950	47.1
1955	43.2
1960	37.9
1965	31.2
1970	29.5

Source: American Transit Association, *Transit Fact Book Supplement,* December 1966).

Frequent strikes and the acute financial problems of the industry produced a period of extraordinarily bitter labor relations in the late 1940s and early 1950s.

Viewed from the labor perspective, real wages *per employee* increased only 13 percent during the eight years from 1946 to 1954, hardly an excessive improvement in the average worker's standard of living considering the buying power that labor surrendered during the war years.[125] But from a management perspective, the settlements of this same period increased real wages *per vehicle mile* by 18 percent, a punishing increase in unit labor costs. Moreover, payroll expense per vehicle mile was increasing 63 percent in current dollars while consumer prices were increasing only 38 percent. Stated still another way, *per passenger* payroll expenses increased 141 percent in current dollars from 1946 to 1954, while operating income per passenger declined 43 percent.[126]

Thus an impasse: the average transit worker's take-home pay increased only modestly during the postwar period while the industry's wage bill increased dramatically from 51 to 60 percent of operating revenues.[127] This apparent anomaly is explained by the industry's declining productivity. Passengers per vehicle mile declined from 7.1 in 1946 to only 4.9 in 1954.[128] Labor costs, of course, are closely related to the vehicle miles of service afforded and the obligation to provide peak-hour capacity, whereas operating revenues are determined by the number of passengers carried. Thus selectively declining patronage and modest wage increases combined in vicelike fashion to drive transit toward insolvency. Such was the industry's financial condition when Congress took up the debate over federal aid for public transportation.

THE PERIOD OF RECOVERY WITHOUT STABILIZATION

Only a handful of cities provided municipal tax subsidies for the operation of transit systems when Congress began debating the issue of federal assistance in 1960.[129] In most cities, private ownership remained the norm, and even in those 38 cities where public acquisition had occurred, most transit operations were managed as public enterprises expected to recover the full expense of day-to-day operation from passenger revenues. Among the nation's major cities, only New York, Newark, San Francisco, Oakland, New Orleans, and Seattle afforded transit service more extensive than could be operated with the revenue generated by passenger fares.[130] One other city, Philadelphia, was experimenting with tax-subsidized commuter railroad service. Thus, local indifference rather than local commitment was the norm when Congress first scheduled hearings on the financial problems of public transportation.

The initiative to obtain federal participation in transit finance did not come from the transit industry per se but from a coalition of big-city mayors and railroad presidents concerned, respectively, about the erosion of commuter service and financial burden that commuter service losses were imposing on railroad freight operations.[131] Thus the debate over federal aid was imprinted from the beginning with a big-city, commuter-rail perspective, although the transit industry was dominated by properties operating bus service in mixed traffic. The mayors and their railroad allies were successful in obtaining a congressional forum for their concerns, but it was leadership from within Congress itself, rather than broadbased constituency pressure, that galvanized congressional support for federal participation in transit finance.[132] We emphasize this point because it illuminates an important matter of historical sequence: federal initiative *preceded* local concern about the future of transit in most communities; indeed, the congressional supporters of transit assistance argued that federal involvement was necessary to motivate and stimulate state and local action in an arena heretofore neglected. Congress was, in short, "out front" of local officialdom and transit management in embracing the proposition that transit should be financed as a public service rather than as a private industry or a public enterprise.

This sequence of events—first federal involvement, then local commitment—had important consequences. It meant that federal aid for transit would become available before local officialdom had grappled either intellectually or financially with the economic problems of public transportation. It meant that intergovernmental grants would become available before localities had given serious study to service options and mobility needs. It meant that there was only a slim body of local administrative experience on which to base the design and thrust of the federal aid program itself—experience limited to a very few cities with populations much larger and denser than the metropolitan norm. And it meant that local officials could not draw on the experience of localities elsewhere as they made plans for public acquisition and service improvement, simply because few communities had such experience. In the process, the conversion from private to public ownership would be forgone as an opportunity to reorganize services, restructure fares, and renegotiate work rules. Properties would pass from private to public ownership carrying with them all the accumulated baggage of contract agreements, service obligations, and pricing rules that had weighed down private operations since the 1920s.

In this sense, federal involvement in transit finance was a kind of mixed blessing. It rescued transit from local inertia and neglect by galvanizing public concern about the preservation of service. But it also precipitated an unstudied local response, as civic leaders made hasty plans to assume public ownership and avail themselves of federal funds. The result can be characterized as recovery without stabilization.

Federal grants and the local financial contribution required of potential grant recipients fundamentally changed the financing of mass transit, shifting the burden of capitalization from the farebox to the public treasury.[133] Capitalization through retained earnings would be replaced by capitalization through tax subsidy and intergovernmental transfer payments, permitting the replacement of aging plant and equipment on an accelerated basis. Although capital grants did not reverse the trend of declining ridership, they did engage state and local governments in financing transit and thus laid the groundwork for service improvements, operating subsidies, and fare stabilization policies that would arrest the loss of ridership. Conversion to public operation and the engagement of localities in transit finance were, indeed, the most important result and the most lasting consequence of the federal aid program.

From 1965 to 1974, federal authorities would disburse almost $3.3 billion in capital grant funds to purchase transit properties from private owners, replace aging fleets, rehabilitate plant and equipment, and build and equip new rapid transit systems. During this period, the number of publicly owned systems increased from 58 to 308.[134] Transit systems across the nation used federal funds to replace aging bus fleets, and the first cycle of fleet replacement had been virtually accomplished by the early 1970s.[135] Despite the infusion of new capital, both transit ridership and service delivered continued to decline from the 1964 inception of the capital grant program through 1972. With fares increasing and service volume in decline, reequipping the industry was insufficient to prevent the 21 percent loss of ridership that occurred from 1964 to 1972.[136]

Transit and the Ferment of the 1960s and 1970s

With ridership and service declining, the early 1970s marked a period of intellectual disarray and organizational crisis for mass transit. Remedies promised to revitalize the industry were not working; worse still, the industry's best efforts to achieve recovery were culminating in financially counterproductive results, as they had in the 1920s. At this critical juncture, a series of loosely related events converged to vest transit with new social imperative, a broader political constituency—and a happier but historically inaccurate explanation for its financial distress. The events to which we are referring include the ghetto riots of the late 1960s, the publication of the Kerner Commission report, and the assassination of Martin Luther King, Jr., all of which gave imperative to solving the problems of urban poverty; the publication of Paul Ehrlich's *The Population Bomb* with its Malthusian vision of environmental degradation; the celebration of Earth Day, a media event that further crystallized environmental concerns; the passage of the Clean Air Act amendments of 1970 that obligated localities to meet federal air pollution standards; the Arab oil embargo of 1972–1973, which created instant public awareness of the energy crisis and the tenuousness of international petroleum supply; the coming of the "freeway revolt" to Boston and the involvement of Harvard and M.I.T. academicians in the advocacy planning it spawned; and the publication of Bradford Snell's *American Ground Transportation*, a vehemently argued account of transit's destruction by General Motors. In combination, these events dramatically increased the social and political salience of urban poverty, the costs of sprawl, and the limits to growth.

Awareness of urban and environmental problems interacted with the activism and disillusionment of the Vietnam era to create what some have called a "consciousness revolution"—a reappraisal of the merits growth, auto-mobility, suburban living, and, more broadly, the appropriateness of *laissez-faire* capitalism as a response to poverty and other urban problems.[137] While "the consciousness revolution" had little effect on spending behavior or consumer choices, it influenced public policy in fundamental ways—including the perception of mass transit. Transit was transformed from a failing industry to a vital public service that should play a central role in shaping urban growth, revitalizing central cities and urban neighborhoods, preserving open space, conserving energy, and reducing automotive pollution. Transit was simultaneously vested with an emotionally compelling apology for its competitive failure: it was the victim of industrial conspiracy and a casualty of misguided and unbalanced public policy. It followed logically that transit's recovery would require the subsidy of day-to-day operations—an expenditure necessary to countervail highway spending and the past biases of public policy.

Thus, the intellectual ferment of the 1960s and early 1970s laid the groundwork for transit operating subsidies, subsidies for the day-to-day operation of service at fares lower than those required to pay operating expenses. While capital grants represented an implicit operating subsidy, explicit subsidy of day-to-day operation was not the industry norm until the 1970s; indeed, passenger fares paid for 82 percent of the industry's current operating expenses as late as 1970.[138] Federal operating assistance was authorized in 1974, and by 1975, passenger fares paid only half the nation's transit operating bill; their contribution had fallen to 38 percent by 1980.[139] In the latter year, local assistance accounted for 47 percent of the governmental operating subsidy made available to transit, whereas federal and state subsidies accounted for 30 percent and 23 percent, respectively.[140]

Operating subsidy and reduced fares arrested the decline of patronage and stimulated ridership increases from 1972 to 1980, but it is impossible to conclude that subsidies have restored transit to stable financial footing. Subsidies permitted an aggregate nationwide increase in service of 9.8 percent from 1970 to 1976, but during the same period, the service afforded by the 10 largest transit properties for which reliable data are available declined by the same amount, namely 9.8 percent.[141] The identity of these statistics is coincidental; what they demonstrate is that intergovernmental subsidies permitted the introduction and expansion of transit service in suburban markets and in small cities without arresting the erosion of service in many of the nation's cities where transit is most essential.

Nor did subsidy provide an incentive or obligation to grapple with the economics of peaking and the corresponding obsolescence of the industry's work rules, craft structure, and pricing policies, a subject we will discuss in some detail in the next chapter. As a result, the per rider cost of providing transit service increased much faster than did the revenues generated by the recovery of patronage that occurred after 1972. The real cost per passenger increased 79 percent from 1965 to 1975 and then declined two percentage points from 1975 to 1980 as rising gasoline prices encouraged motorists to use public transportation.[142] If we factor out the effect of higher gasoline prices and the mode shift it produced, a 25 percent increase in subsidy was necessary to achieve a 13 percent increase in ridership from 1975 to 1980.[143]

Table 3-16 shows the recent trend of transit ridership and the corresponding trend of cost and subsidy per ride. Figure 3-1 shows the trend of cost per passenger mile and per seat mile. The inescapable con-

TABLE 3-16   Estimated Transit Industry Performance,
Selected Years, 1965–1980

Year	Ridership (billions)	Cost per Ride (1967 dollars)	Subsidy per Ride (1967 dollars)
1965	8.3	18.4 cents	1.4 cents
1970	7.3	22.4	4.4
1975	7.0	32.9	16.6
1980	8.2	32.1	19.9

Source: Data reported in American Public Transit Association *Transit Fact Book* (New York, APTA, 1981).

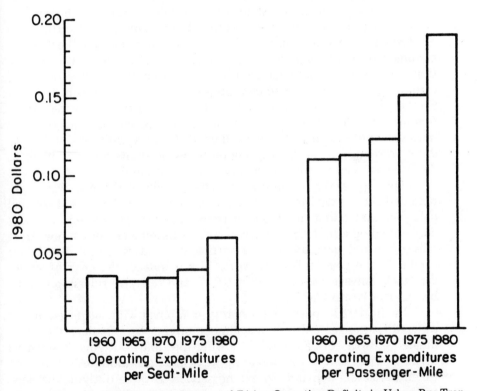

Source: Don H. Pickrell, "The Sources of Rising Operating Deficits in Urban Bus Transit," in Transportation Research Record 915 (Washington, D.C.: Transportation Research Board, 1983).

Figure 3-1 Trends in Unit Expenditures and Revenues for U.S. Bus Transit Operations, 1960–1980

clusion is that enormous subsidy was required to reverse the decline of patronage and that ever-increasing subsidy has been necessary to sustain that recovery. This does not bode well for transit's future, because an industry that requires ever-increasing subsidy is not one that has been restored to a stable economic footing.

A BRIEF SUMMARY

We have shown that transit's decline was a complex phenomenon rooted in the developmental history of street railways. The industry's developmental years damaged its credit and, perhaps more important, encumbered transit with service obligations, a fare structure, work rules, and a maze of cross-subsidies that crippled the industry's ability to adjust to the competition of the automobile.

Traction companies lost investor confidence early in the century because of the speculative excesses that accompanied the electrification of street railways. The industry's credit was also damaged because its earning power was impaired by fixed fares and rising costs. Cost escalation was caused by both general inflation and punitive regulation. Weak earnings forced many small-city properties into receivership or bankruptcy before the advent of automotive competition. Impaired profit potential also led to disinvestment on the part of another class of street railways—those owned by consolidated utilities with the ability to divert revenues from railway depreciation accounts and use them as development capital for light and power operations.

The cost-revenue squeeze in street railway finance was compounded by the decisions of the War Labor Board. The board reached decisions that raised the wages of transit workers without ensuring any corresponding adjustment in fares. As a consequence, only a few street railways could generate profits sufficient to attract new investment capital in the years following World War I. Indeed, the peak of street-car track mileage was reached in 1917, and selective ridership decline began after World War I.

In the 1920s, postwar prosperity combined with the development of credit arrangements for installment buying to stimulate the coordinate growth of automobile ownership and outlying residential districts. Prior to the war, street railways had been more or less successful in deflecting demands to extend service to these outlying districts. In the postwar period, the introduction of the gasoline-powered motorbus and its operation by independent companies generated new pressure to extend service to outlying districts. Street railways responded preemptively to what was seen as a competitive threat, acquiring independent bus lines and extending service to suburban territory.

Suburban extensions further depressed profit margins, and sustaining suburban services required cross-subsidies between long- and short-haul riders. Short-haul ridership was also discouraged by the successive fare increases sought and obtained during the postwar period. Thus, the attenuation of service and increases in the base fare eroded the industry's primary economic base—the short-haul market.

The postwar diffusion of the automobile was sufficient to destroy the already thin patronage base of transit operations in the smaller cities of the farmbelt and mountain states. Indeed, automobile sales were first concentrated in cities of this class. Many such properties terminated operation in the 1920s.

In larger cities, the growth of automobile ownership and usage eroded transit ridership selectively, and the first competition between the two modes can be characterized as oblique. Automobile owners abandoned the use of transit for touring, shopping trips, group travel, and other off-peak travel purposes. Because of the increasing imbalance between peak and off-peak demand, efforts to expand service to compete with the automobile increased commuter patronage but reduced profit margins further.

With transit's expansion effectively stymied, the automobile and highway shaped the patterns of urban development and the geography of urban travel from the 1920s onward. Without growth potential, transit management focused its attention on cost reduction as its primary strategy of economic recovery. Both labor and service were reduced in the effort to shed costs. Service reductions eroded ridership further, and wage concessions necessary to obtain union agreement to labor reductions limited the effectiveness of economy measures on the labor front.

Wage rates continued to be negotiated on the basis of parity with manufacturing workers despite the industry's declining ridership and declining productivity. As a consequence, further cost shedding and higher fares were needed to pay the industry's wage bill and avert strikes.

As profit margins declined, street railways were unable to generate earnings sufficient to replace track and rolling stock or to upgrade equipment. Conversion to buses occurred as a matter of financial necessity. Conversion began in the 1920s, accelerated during the depression, and continued through the 1950s. Operating substitute bus service allowed street railways to reduce short-term capital costs, but at the expense of higher long-term operating costs. Flexibility in routing was also gained, but economies of density were sacrificed.

The depression caused wholesale loss of ridership and precipitated rapid disinvestment as the industry shed service and equipment in an emergency effort to reduce costs. During the depression, Congress adopted legislation establishing the 40-hour, five-day workweek as the national norm. The measure was intended to spread employment opportunity, but it served to reduce transit's Saturday patronage base. Depression-era antitrust legislation also affected mass transit by obliging electric utilities to divest their electric traction operations. This compromised the ability of some properties to obtain capital at favorable interest rates. But in other cases, divestiture only ended a corporate marriage that had soured long before.

The exigencies of World War II—gas and tire rationing, the suspension of automobile production, and the growth of employment associated with war production—produced a resurgence of transit patronage. The wartime ridership crest cannot be interpreted as evidence of an industry operating at the peak of its performance; it must instead be seen as an artifact of wartime conservation measures, travel by servicemen, and the unusually high employment levels generated by war production. The exigencies of war increased transit ridership to levels that could not be sustained in the postwar period, and precipitous loss of patronage accompanied the return to normalcy.

National policies designed to buffer the transition from war production to civilian employment would engage the federal government in large-scale spending for public works. The first federal spending for urban highways occurred during the depression and was conceived as a job-creating measure. Plans for postwar public works engaged state highway department in urban highway planning on a permanent basis. The urban highways built by the states in the postwar period were designed to much higher standards than were those built in earlier years by cities and counties. State highways were designed for high speeds and scaled to accommodate peak-hour traffic volumes. The performance capabilities of freeways and the method used in financing them prevented trunkline transit operations from adopting higher peak-hour fares as a strategy to increase revenues while accommodating increasingly unbalanced load factors.

Freeway construction had its most direct competitive impact on railroad commuter operations and rapid transit systems—the growth sector of the public transportation industry in the late 1920s. The impact of freeway construction on surface lines would be more oblique. The enormous traffic volumes delivered to central business districts by radial freeways would impede bus and streetcar operations, further attenuating headways and further discouraging short-distance ridership. Thus, freeway development further compounded the traffic imbalance of transit systems—eroding the off-peak ridership of trunk rail facilities and the short-haul ridership of city services. In the postwar period, an exhausted and demoralized industry pursued contraction as the only feasible response to precipitously declining ridership and revenues. As in the 1920s, the loss of patronage was selective. Transit properties lost the weekend, midday, and countercommuter traffic that once produced the revenue necessary to counterbalance the high cost of providing the capacity and labor necessary to serve the rush-hour peak.

Declining service, ridership, and revenues prompted a reappraisal of the appropriateness of private ownership as the mode of operation for public transportation, but by 1960, only a handful of transit systems in largest cities had been acquired by public service districts. Publicly owned systems were typically managed on a full-cost recovery basis and did not operate with reduced fares.

Such was the state of the industry when Congress first debated the merits of providing federal aid for urban mass transportation. The congressional supporters of federal subsidy argued that federal intervention was necessary to galvanize state and local involvement in an arena heretofore neglected. Federal aid produced this result—rapid conversion of the transit industry from private to public ownership and a dramatic shift in the source of industry revenues. Tax subsidy replaced farebox revenue as the industry's primary revenue source and the decline of patronage was arrested as subsidy increased. Subsidy permitted fare stabilization and a mild recovery in ridership, but transit has continued to lose market share, and steadily increasing subsidy has been necessary to sustain the recovery of ridership. Thus, subsidy has not stabilized the industry's financial position, and periodic financial crises have buffeted the industry since public ownership became the norm.

As this summary indicates, distress and instability has characterized public transportation for most of the twentieth century. Subsidy has not stabilized the industry, and sustaining service and patronage would require ever-increasing tax support.

Our recapitulation describes the sequence of events that led to transit's decline but still leaves unanswered the equally important question: Why has the industry been unable to adjust to the forces of decline and find a workable strategy of reorganization and renewal?

Our answer to this question will reveal that, in a very fundamental sense, instability continues as a result of the industry's inability to adjust to significant changes in the composition of its ridership and the balance of its traffic that have rendered its fare structure, its wage structure, its work rules, and its routing philosophy increasingly obsolete.

NOTES

1. Quoted in Edward S. Mason, *The Street Railway in Massachusetts* (Cambridge, Mass.: Harvard University Press, 1932), p. 10.

2. Institute of Public Administration, *Financing Transit: Alternatives for*

Local Government (Washington, D.C.: U.S. Department of Transportation, 1979), pp. 1-3.

3. U.S. Bureau of the Census, *Street and Electric Railways, 1902* (Washington, D.C.: Government Printing Office, 1905), pp. 126-148.

4. Ibid., pp. 54-93.

5. Emerson P. Schmidt, *Industrial Relations in Urban Transportation* (Minneapolis: University of Minnesota Press, 1937), pp. 102-149.

6. Ibid., pp. 102-117.

7. Leo Wolman, *Ebb and Flow in Trade Unionism* (New York: National Bureau of Economic Research, 1936), p. 118.

8. Schmidt, *Industrial Relations in Urban Transportation*, pp. 51-61.

9. Census Bureau, *Street Railways, 1902*, p. 6.

10. Ibid.

11. F. W. Doolittle, *Studies in the Cost of Urban Transportation Service* (New York: American Electric Railway Association, 1916), p. 12.

12. Delos F. Wilcox, *Analysis of the Electric Railway Problem* (published by the author, 1921), pp. 36-39.

13. Ibid., p. 38.

14. Ibid.

15. U.S. Bureau of the Census, *Street and Electric Railways, 1907* (Washington, D.C.: Government Printing Office, 1910), pp. 100-103.

16. Ibid., p. 123.

17. See for example, O. E. Carson, *The Trolley Titans* (Glendale, Calif.: Interurban Press, 1921), pp. 21-51.

18. John I. Beggs, "Address of the President," *Proceedings, 1907* (American Street and Interurban Railway Association), pp. 63-65.

19. Ibid., pp. 63-65, and Calvin G. Goodrich, "Address of the President," *Proceedings, 1908* (American Street and Interurban Railway Association), p. 101.

20. Richard Solomon and Arthur Saltzman, "Historical Overview of the Decline of the Transit Industry," *Highway Research Record*, No. 417 (1972), pp. 4-5.

21. American Electric Railway Association, *The Urban Transportation Problem* (New York: AERA, circa 1933), p. 16.

22. Doolittle, *The Cost of Urban Transportation*, pp. 35-56.

23. Goodrich, *1908 ASIRA Proceedings*, p. 101.

24. Ibid., and Schmidt, *Industrial Relations in Urban Transportation*, pp. 33-35.

25. Melvile J. Ulmer, *Capital in Transportation, Communications and Public Utilities* (Princeton, N.J.: Princeton University Press, 1960), pp. 405-406.

26. Census Bureau, *Street Railways, 1907*, p. 23.

27. Ibid., pp. 38-50.

28. Ibid.

29. Ibid., p. 129.

30. Blakemore Analytical Reports, *The Public Utilities: A Retrospection and Forecast to 1930* (New York: BAR, 1926), pp. 3-14.

31. Ulmer, *Capital in Transportation*, pp. 405-406.

32. U.S. Bureau of the Census, *Electric Railways and Affiliated Motor Bus Lines, 1927* (Washington: Government Printing Office, 1931), p. 5.

33. Schmidt, *Industrial Relations in Urban Transportation*, p. 50.

34. See Doolittle, *The Cost of Urban Transportation*, pp. 35-56.

35. Schmidt, *Industrial Relations in Urban Transportation*, pp. 102-106.

36. Ibid., pp. 210-212.

37. Ibid., p. 161.

38. U.S. Bureau of the Census, *Historical Statistics of the United States* (Washington, D.C.: Government Printing Office, 1976), p. 210.

39. Alexander M. Bing, *War-time Strikes and Their Adjustment* (New York: E. P. Dutton, 1921), Appendix I.

40. Ibid.

41. Ibid.

42. Ibid.

43. Schmidt, *Industrial Relations in Urban Transportation*, pp. 159-163.

44. Ibid., p. 211.

45. Quoted in Ibid., p. 161.

46. American Electric Railway Association, *The Urban Transportation Problem*, p. 6.

47. Ibid.

48. Ibid., pp. 6-11.

49. Wolman, *Trade Unionism*, p. 118.

50. National Automobile Chamber of Commerce, USA, *Facts and Figures of the Automobile Industry, 1928* (New York: NACC, 1928), p. 11.

51. Alain Kornhauser and Lawrence Wilson, "Role of New Technology in Urban Transportation" (unpublished manuscript, circa 1975), unpaginated.

52. U.S. Bureau of the Census, *Electric Railways, 1917* (Washington, D.C.: Government Printing Office, 1920), p. 68.

53. Blakemore Reports, *The Public Utilities*, pp. 20-22.

54. James J. Flink, *American Adopts the Automobile, 1895-1910* (Cambridge, Mass.: M.I.T. Press, 1970), pp. 69-70, 84-85.

55. George W. Hilton and John F. Due, *The Electric Interurban Railways in America* (Stanford, Calif.: Stanford University Press, 1960), pp. 93-96.

56. Robert S. Lynd and Helen N. Lynd, *Middletown* (New York: Harcourt, Brace, 1929), pp. 253-254.

57. Estimated from data reported in Census Bureau, *Electric Railways, 1927*, pp. 11, 99.

58. Solomon and Saltzman, "Decline of the Transit Industry," p. 5.

59. Census Bureau, *Street Railways, 1907*, p. 129.

60. Blakemore Reports, *The Public Utilities*, p. 117.

61. Ibid., p. 117.

62. Ibid., pp. 117-119.

63. American Electric Railway Association, *Proceedings, 1925* (New York: AERA), p. 194.

64. Automobile Chamber of Commerce, *Facts and Figures, 1927*, p. 38.

65. A theme stated repeatedly in the *Proceedings* of the American Electric Railway Association during the mid- and late 1920s.

66. See Table 2-5 on page 23.

67. Doolittle, *The Cost of Urban Transportation*, pp. 37–46.

68. George M. Graham, "The Motor Vehicle—Competitor or Ally?" in *AERA Proceedings, 1920* (New York: American Electric Railway Association), p. 327.

69. L. H. Palmer, "Are These High Costs of Service Likely to Develop Permanent Competition?" in *The Proceedings of the American Electric Railway Association*, 1919, p. 284.

70. Graham, *AERA Proceedings, 1920*, p. 327.

71. James D. Mortimer, chairman of the Committee on (Convention) Subjects, 1920 convention of the American Electric Railway Association, *AERA Proceedings, 1920*, p. 317.

72. "Report of the Committee on Trackless Transportation," *Proceedings, 1923* (New York: American Electric Railway Association), p. 127.

73. Automobile Chamber of Commerce, *Facts and Figures, 1926*, p. 31.

74. Graham, *AERA Proceedings, 1920*, p. 318.

75. Ibid., p. 319.

76. "Passengers Carried by United States Transit Operators, 1890-1935," *Transit Journal*, January 1936, p. 6.

77. Palmer, *AERA Proceedings, 1919*, p. 285.

78. "Electric Railway Operations in 1925," *AERA*, May 1926, p. 5.

79. R. H. Pinkley, "How the Industry Is Progressing," *AERA Proceedings, 1927* (New York: American Electric Railway Association), pp. 127-129.

80. American Electric Railway Association, *The Urban Transportation Problem*, p. 11.

81. Ibid., pp. 35–36.

82. Ibid., p. 36; Francis R. Thompson, *Electric Transportation* (Scranton, Pa.: International Textbook Company, 1940), pp. 45–49.

83. Ibid., p. 12.

84. Ibid., p. 11.

85. American Transit Association, *Transit Industry of the U.S.* (New York: ATA, 1943), p. 10.

86. George Krambles, "Trolley Buses from Management's Point of View," Transportation Research Board Trolley Bus Workshop, Seattle, Washington, August 1982, pp. 2–6.

87. American Transit Association, Committee on Bus Equipment and Maintenance, "Diesel Engines and Equipment" (New York: ATA, 1940), p. 5.

88. Bradford F. Snell, Senate Judiciary Committee, *American Ground Transportation* (Washington, D.C.: Government Printing Office, 1974), p. 32.

89. American Transit Association, "Diesel Equipment," p. 5.

90. Snell, *American Ground Transportation*, pp. 28–35.

91. Seymour Adler, *The Political Economy of Transit in the San Francisco Bay Area, 1945-63* (Berkeley: University of California, Institute of Urban and Personal Development, 1980), pp. 61–62.

92. Krambles, *Trolley Buses*, p. 2.

93. Jonathan Gifford, "An Analysis of the Federal Role in the Planning, Design and Deployment of Rural Highways, Toll Roads, and Urban Freeways" (Unpublished Ph.D. thesis, University of California, Berkeley, 1983), Chap. 3.

94. David W. Jones, Jr., "Urban Highway Investment and the Political Economy of Fiscal Retrenchment," in Alan A. Altshuler, ed., *Current Issues in Transportation Policy* (New York: Heath-Lexington, 1979), pp. 69-70.

95. Norman Hebden and Wilbur S. Smith, *State-City Relationships in Highway Affairs* (New Haven, Conn.: Yale University Press, 1950), pp. 36-46.

96. See, for example, the *Second Biennial Report* of the California Highway Commission (Sacramento: California State Printing Office, 1921), p. 9.

97. Thomas H. MacDonald, "Federal Aid from the National Viewpoint," a paper presented at the 1944 convention of the American Association of State Highway Officials, Cincinnati, Ohio, 1944, p. 29; Charles M. Noble, "The Modern Express Highway," in *Transactions* of the American Society of Civil Engineers, Vol. 102 (1937), p. 1069.

98. U.S. Public Roads Administration, *Public Control of Highway Access and Roadside Development* (Washington, D.C.: Government Printing Office, 1947), pp. 3-7.

99. MacDonald, "Federal Aid from the National Viewpoint," p. 29; Noble, "The Modern Express Highway," p. 1069.

100. National Transportation Policy Study Commission, *National Transportation Policies Through the Year 2000* (Washington, D.C.: Government Printing Office, 1979), p. 227; Kirin Bhatt, *An Analysis of Road Expenditures and Payments by Vehicle Class (1956-1975)* (Washington, D.C.: The Urban Institute, 1977), p. 69.

101. A conclusion derived from reviewing postwar highway plans proposed by municipal and traffic engineering officials in *metropolitan areas* where states developed ambitious freeway systems: Detroit, Los Angeles, and San Francisco. See also John Nolan and Henry V. Hubbard, *Parkways and Land Values* (Cambridge, Mass.: Harvard University Press, 1937), pp. 106-119.

102. Wilbur Smith, *Future Highways and Urban Growth* (Detroit: The Automobile Manufacturers Association, 1961), p. 180.

103. William S. Vickrey, "Economic Efficiency and Pricing," in Selma Mushkin, ed., *Public Prices for Public Products* (Washington, D.C.: The Urban Institute, 1972), pp. 67-68.

104. This is precisely the outcome highway officials warned would occur if freeway development outpaced local traffic management, parking management and transit service adjustments. See "Development of Major New Facilities," in *Traffic Engineering Functions and Administration* (Chicago: Public Information Service, 1948), pp. 99-104. See also Public Roads Administration, *Interregional Highways* (Washington, D.C.: Government Printing Office, 1944), pp. 76-79.

Transit operation in mixed vehicular traffic was frequently cited as problematic in the transit trade press during the postwar period. See, for example, Sidney H. Bingham, "Traffic and Operations," *Mass Transportation*, September 1950, pp. 48-49.

105. J. R. Meyer, J. F. Kain, and M. Wohl, *The Urban Transportation Problem* (Cambridge, Mass.: Harvard University Press, 1965), Chaps. 3 and 6.

106. David W. Jones, Jr., "The Cost-Revenue Squeeze in Conventional Transit Finance," in *Transportation Research Board Special Report*, No. 184 (Washington, D.C.: Transportation Research Board, 1979), p. 60.

107. Sar A. Levitan and Richard S. Belous, *Shorter Hours, Shorter Weeks* (Baltimore: The Johns Hopkins University Press, 1977), p. 7.

108. Saltzman and Solomon, "Decline of the Transit Industry," p. 44-45.

109. Public Administration Clearing House, *Transit Facts* (Washington, D.C.: PACH, 1955), p. 1.

110. Ibid., p. 10.

111. Ibid., p. 4.

112. Ibid., p. 10.

113. Ibid., p. 4.

114. Meyer, Kain, and Wohl, *The Urban Transportation Problem*, Chap. 1.

115. Ibid., Chap. 3.

116. George Hilton, "The Decline of Railroad Commutation," *The Business History Review*, Summer 1962, p. 174.

117. Howard Hosmer, "Railroad Passenger Train Deficit" (Washington, D.C.: Interstate Commerce Commission, 1958), Docket No. 31954, Sheets 50-52.

118. *Report of the Transit Commissioner*, Volume II (Philadelphia: Transit Commission, 1913), Map 42.

119. American Electric Railway Association, *The Urban Transportation Problem*, p. 15.

120. The debate over public ownership began in earnest in 1951 with the publication of "The Bingham Formula" by Sidney H. Bingham, *Mass Transportation*, August 1951, p. 21. See also "The Bingham Formula Begins to Roll," *Mass Transportation*, December 1951, p. 17.

121. Ohio-Kentucky-Indiana Regional Planning Authority, *Profile of Selected Mass Transit Operations in the United States* (Cincinnati: OKIRPA, 1969), p. 43.

122. Ibid., pp. 43-44.

123. Estimated from data reported in the American Public Transit Association, *Transit Fact Book, 1981* (Washington, D.C.: APTA, 1981), p. 43.

124. Public Administration Clearing House, *Transit Facts*, p. 5.

125. Ibid.

126. Ibid.

127. Ibid.

128. Ibid.

129. American Transit Association, *Transit Operating Reports—1960* (New York: ATA, 1961), pp. 2-5.

130. Ibid.

131. Michael N. Danielson, *Federal-Metropolitan Politics and the Commuter Crisis* (New York: Columbia University Press, 1965), pp. 95-106.

132. Ibid., pp. 130-131.

133. Institute of Public Administration, *Financing Transit: Alternatives for Local Government* (Washington, D.C.: U.S. Department of Transportation, 1979), pp. 14-17.

134. American Public Transit Association, *Transit Fact Book, 1981*, p. 43.

135. Institute of Public Administration, *Financing Transit*, p. 17.

136. American Public Transit Association, *'72-'73 Transit Fact Book*, p. 8.

137. See, for example, Charles A. Reich, *The Greening of America* (New

York: Random House, 1970), and Richard N. Goodwin, *The American Condition* (Garden City, N.Y.: Doubleday, 1974).

138. American Public Transit Association, *Transit Fact Book, 1981*, pp. 46-47.

139. Ibid.

140. Ibid.

141. Estimated from data reported in *Transit Operating Reports* published by the American Transit Association and its successor the American Public Transit Association in 1971 and 1977.

142. Estimated from data reported in American Public Transit Association, *Transit Fact Book, 1981*, pp. 47 and 52. See also p. 59.

143. The transit ridership attributable to the volatility of gasoline prices and supplies was calculated as a residual after accounting for the effects of reduced fares and increased service. These effects were computed using fare and service elasticities reported in *Patronage Impacts of Changes in Transit Fares and Services* (Washington, D.C.: U.S. Department of Transportation, 1980) and levels of fares and service reported in the *Transit Fact Book, 1981*.

4

THE DYNAMICS OF TRANSIT'S DECLINE AND CONTINUING DISTRESS

INTRODUCTION

In a very fundamental sense, it is impossible to understand fully the dynamics of transit's decline without understanding why the industry has been unable to find a workable strategy of stabilization and renewal. In short, Why was transit unable to adapt to the competition of the automobile and thus establish a foundation for recovery and renewed growth? And why has it required steadily *increasing* subsidy, once the opportunity to obtain subsidy was afforded?

The answer to each of these questions is imbedded in the history, customs, and politics of the industry. Transit has been unable to reorganize, recoup, and thereby achieve financial stability because its developmental years encumbered the industry with pricing customs, operating conventions, a craft structure, a wage scale, and routing philosophy that are out of date. The industry continues to operate with customs and traditions inherited from the era in which transit was the dominant form of mechanized urban transportation. Those customs and traditions are incompatible with its current role in the urban transportation system—a role that is subordinate and supplemental to that of the automobile.

Both the practices and the structure of the transit industry have proven resistant to change because organized constituencies have possessed the political influence necessary to protect entitlements vested by custom and usage. The most important of these constituencies are transit riders, transit labor, and the downtown growth establishment. Each group has been successful in protecting the erosion of a privilege that it perceives as a rightful entitlement:

1. Labor: That wages should increase in a manner that allows transit workers to make modest, but steady, improvement in their standard of living.
2. Passengers: That fares should remain essentially constant.
3. The growth establishment: That peak-hour capacity should be preserved as a commitment to the health of the downtown economy.

These are not inherently wrongheaded, unreasonable, or excessive expectations, but they have interacted with inflation, the industry's structure and the changing composition of transit's ridership base to frustrate recovery and cause continuing financial distress. Stated another way, the industry's structure and the composition of its residual traffic do not permit these expectations to be honored without recurrent financial crisis or steadily increasing tax support.

In the pages that follow, we shall see how four factors have worked together to cause continuing financial distress: (1) the changing composition of transit's ridership base, (2) the obsolescence of the industry's basic structure, (3) felt obligations to organized constituencies, and (4) the impact of general inflation. We will discuss each in turn.

THE CHANGING COMPOSITION OF TRANSIT'S RIDERSHIP BASE

In its developmental years, the street railway was the dominant medium of urban transportation. The service it provided was used by people of all means, all backgrounds, and all ages. In these early years, transit functioned as a general-purpose transportation utility, serving the full spectrum of travel purposes: shopping trips, excursion travel, and family recreation travel as well as the journey to work. Because transit served a broad spectrum of travel needs, the demand for rush-hour service was balanced by travel that occurred at midday, on weekends, and during the early evening hours.[1] Because even the largest cities were relatively small in scale, the demand for service was spatially concentrated. The spatial concentration and temporal diffusion of the demand for transit service combined to produce a pattern of traffic with both sufficient density and sufficient balance to permit profitable operation in a large number of cities.

In the modern American city, transit is a subordinate form of transportation that plays a role that is supplemental to the automobile's. Transit dominates the automobile in only one travel submarket—journeys to and from work in central business districts where parking is scarce and costly. Even the so-called "transit dependent"—the poor, the elderly, and the physically disabled—typically use transit as a supplement to travel by car. Few "transit dependents" are truly carless in the sense that they are unable to share in the auto-mobility of friends, neighbors, or relatives. While many are ride-reliant, few are solely dependent on public transportation for personal mobility.[2]

The growth of American cities and the selective loss of ridership have resulted in a pattern of demand that is spatially attenuated and temporally concentrated. This is the obverse of the traffic pattern that prevailed when transit properties were profitable ventures. Transit continues to operate, however, with pricing rules, a fare structure, and work rules that were appropriate to the period when demand was spatially concentrated and temporally diffuse.

The Obsolescence of Transit's Fare Structure

During its developmental years, the transit industry adopted pricing customs that were appropriate to the markets then served. Regular riders who used transit for their daily journey to work were afforded discount fares, a marketing strategy suited to encouraging riding by those who would otherwise walk to work. A flat fare was charged regardless of the distance traveled, because routes were typically only 3 to 5 miles long.

By dint of usage, these privileges became established as customs and eventually as rightful entitlements. Thus, today's rider expects a flat fare that is uniform with distance or, at most, gently tapered. Patrons also expect that fares will be discounted in proportion to the regularity of use. The regular user who rides transit to work and must tolerate the disamenity of a crowded coach deserves a reduced fare—or so custom has it.

These pricing rules continue in the modern era despite fundamental change in the balance and composition of transit's ridership base. Transit's residual ridership is composed primarily of peak-hour commuters—precisely those patrons who are most costly to serve because the capacity requirements of the peak period fix a property's capital costs and its payroll obligations. Serving such riders can be two to five times more costly than carrying patrons who travel at midday.[3]

Carrying high-cost riders over increasingly long distances has become the industry's primary role, a role for which it is ill suited because of the structure of its costs and fares. Indeed, the misfit between transit's residual market and its fare structure is an important explanation for the industry's impaired earning power.

THE OBSOLESCENCE OF THE INDUSTRY'S BASIC ORGANIZATIONAL STRUCTURE

The transit industry's work rules, its craft structure, its wage scales, and the way in which service is stratified are also products of the street railway era. They reflect the economic conditions and the balance of traffic that prevailed at the turn of the century. Thus, the industry's work rules and craft structure are suited to a temporally balanced patronage base in which peak-hour traffic is counterbalanced by midday and weekend ridership. Likewise, its wage scales and promotion customs are better suited to an era of stable prices than to a period of persistent inflation.

Long-established work rules and contract agreements prevent most transit properties from hiring part-time labor, training operators to perform vehicle maintenance during the off-peak, or using mechanics in mixed driving and maintenance roles. In turn, declining off-peak ridership means that a sizable fraction of the typical property's work force must be idled during the midday.[4] Contract agreements usually require the property to pay drivers for an 8-hour day plus so-called "split-shift differentials"; the split-shift differential compensates labor for the extended span of the transit workday, typically 6 A.M. to 6 P.M.[5] The arrangement is problematic because actual driving time may only amount to 4 or 5 hours, although the worker's elapsed-time workday may span 11 to 12 hours. Hiring willing part-time labor would permit a closer fit between the temporal rhythms of supply and demand, but this is precluded by most contract agreements.

Contract agreements also prevent properties from training and using operators as mechanics during the midday hours when many drivers and vehicles are idle. The same provisions preclude any breach of craft specialization that would allow mechanics to drive buses when only one peak-hour run is scheduled for a bus used as a so-called "tripper."

If properties could employ part-time labor, they could realize operating economies in the range of 5 to 10 percent.[6] For larger urban properties, this would be a savings equivalent to the financial relief that was afforded by federal subsidy at the peak of the operating assistance program.[7] More important, part-time labor would position many properties to expand peak-hour service without assuming the cost penalty of split-shift differentials or pay for midday idle time. Unfortunately, transit unions have perceived part-time labor as a threat to the job security of the existing work force and thus have vehemently opposed such proposals. As a consequence, part-time workers account for only 2.5 percent of the industry's labor force.[8]

A much larger but less transparent financial dilemma is posed by the industry's wage scales, career ladders, and service mix. The typical American transit property operates with a wage scale that is extremely compressed. Most transit workers reach the top end of the pay scale after less than two years of employment and many after less than a year.[9] Thus, promotion for merit does not afford an opportunity for transit workers to increase their take-home pay, and increases in the base wage must bear the full burden of improving the transit worker's standard of living. Because transit workers cannot better their standard of living by assuming positions of increasing responsibility and productivity, properties face unrelenting pressure to increase hourly wages at a rate that outpaces inflation and allows workers to "do a little better" each year.

The transit industry's service mix compounds this dynamic. Most properties operate what amounts to only one class of service. There is usually some differentiation between local and express services and between peak and base headways, but these are the typical limits of service differentiation in the American transit industry. This means that labor cannot better its standard of living by promotion from one class of service to another that pays higher wages based on greater productivity; gains for labor hinge on increases in the base wage rate, not on promotions up a service or career ladder.

The uniformity of transit services has a second consequence as well. Operating one class of service conceived in terms of the requirements of peak-hour commutation means that the typical property's vehicle fleet, route structure, cost structure, and mode of operation is ill suited to the off-peak market. The operation of small vehicles in a taxilike demand-responsive mode would allow transit agencies to capture a larger share of the midday travel market. But such operation is incompatible with the work rules, wage levels, and vehicle types with which most properties operate.

What if services were differentiated and wage scales were stratified on a career ladder basis? Transit workers could better their standard of living by promotions to positions of increasing responsibility. If transit offered a broader spectrum of *both* services *and* training opportunities, a career in the industry might take the following path. Entry-level workers might operate conventional bus service on routes characterized by the relative ease of the driving task. After a break-in period, they would be eligible to post up to the operation of a high-capacity articulated coach on densely trafficked routes. Promotion would entail a productivity-based wage increase. Another wage increase could be obtained by posting up to another class of service that entails operation of a minibus in fixed-route service during the rush hour, then providing off-boulevard, demand-responsive service with the same vehicle during the off peak.[10] Still another promotion would be available for operating a coach during the rush hour and entering a maintenance training program during the midday. At the top end of the operator ladder, premium wages would be paid for work roles involving driving tasks during the rush hour and light-duty maintenance tasks during the midday. After establishing journeyman status as a mechanic, operators would be eligible to advance up the maintenance ladder. Some workers would leave the transit industry at this point, preferring the wages and daytime work hours of a trained mechanic in the private sector.

The dilemma with the scenario we have painted is that its implementation would require simultaneous change in transit's work rules, fleet mix, wage scales, operating procedures, and marketing philosophy. It would require, in short, compound change of considerable risk. The risk is worth venturing—at least experimentally—because service differentiation and career ladder stratification would begin the change process necessary to structure services that are compatible with the temporal rhythms of the residual demand for public transportation. It would create incentives for labor to ally itself with a process of technology substitution and service innovation designed to increase productivity. It might diffuse at least some of the pressure to increase base wages, because workers could better their standard of living by advancing to positions of increasing responsibility. And, finally, it could reduce *unit* labor costs yet increase the individual worker's take-home pay.[11]

As we have noted, pressure to increase base wages and the transit industry's service mix are intrinsically interrelated. Transit cannot make better use of idle personnel without developing different kinds of career paths and without diversifying the kinds of services it offers. Conversely, transit cannot diversify its service offerings or provide better long-term career opportunities without changing its work rules, wage structure, and fleet mix. Both management and transit workers are caught on the horns of this dilemma.

Unfortunately, service differentiation and career ladder stratification are foreign to the industry's accustomed world view. Only a handful of properties are comfortable with the marketing philosophy inherent in market segmentation and service differentiation, and thus progress on this front has been painfully slow. It has been retarded further by labor's perception that any transition to a ladder-based promotion system would necessarily entail a loss of jobs and at least a short-term reduction in pay for workers with minimal seniority. As a consequence, properties face unremitting pressure to adjust the base

TABLE 4-1   Structural Aspects of Transit's Financial Distress

The Industry's Structure	The Way It Does Business	The Effect of Structure on Performance
Cost structure	Capital costs and payroll obligations are primarily occasioned by the capacity requirements of the peak.	Increasing peak hour service entails a significant incremental cost.
Craft structure	Responsibility for coach operation and coach maintenance are strictly segregated by formal agreement.	Operating personnel that are idle during the off-peak may not be used in maintenance assignments.
Wage scales and career ladders	Wage scales are compressed and promotion to top-end scales occurs after two years or less.	Transit workers cannot improve their standard of living by advancing to positions of increasing responsibility. The base wage bears virtually the full burden of bettering the transit worker's standard of living.
The structure of service	Most properties operate only one class of service conceived in terms of the requirements of peak-hour commuting.	The vehicles used and their mode of operation are ill suited to the off-peak market.
Network structure	Radial configuration is the industry norm. Network configuration is determined by the geometry of peak hours flows.	The network has limited and accidental utility for off-peak travel.
Fare structure	Fares are uniform with distance and by time of day. *De facto* discounts for peak-hour travel are afforded by the sale of passes or commuter books.	Fares fail to reflect the cost occasioned by peak-hour capacity and routes of attenuated length. Fare increases produce less revenue than would be the case with a differential fare structure because off-peak ridership is more price sensitive than is commuter ridership.

wage upward as the sole available means to better the economic position of the industry's work force.

Table 4-1 summarizes the constellation of factors that has contributed to the industry's structural obsolescence. It shows the many ways in which the supply structure of the industry is incompatible with the pattern of demand that prevails in the automobile era.

FELT OBLIGATIONS TO ORGANIZED CONSTITUENCIES

The development of the street railway industry occurred during a deflationary period in which producer prices declined slowly but steadily. This is a fact of enormous consequence for today's transit industry. With the general price level falling, street railways agreed to franchise convenants that fixed fares at 5 cents. Indeed, the average fare remained constant at 5 cents for almost 30 years from 1890 to 1917.[12] This established the expectation and custom that fares should remain essentially constant. The expectation continues today, with most riders believing that a constant transit fare is a rightful entitlement.

During the deflationary years of the nineteenth century, street railway labor organized to share in the growth of profits produced by a fixed fare and declining cost. Labor adopted the bargaining position that base wages should increase in a fashion that allowed transit workers to make modest but steady improvement in their standard of living.[13] The standard of living afforded by the base wages of the late 1800s was a mean one at the margin of subsistence, and progress toward "a living wage" was, in fact, painfully slow. By 1917, it was the policy of the Amalgamated Transit Union that "there are certain rights of labor, and one of those is the right to a living wage, irrespective of what the cost may be or what the effect may be, and we believe the public will afford it."[14]

The position enunciated in 1917 has continued as the bargaining policy of the two unions that dominate the transit industry, and wage settlements that allow workers to better their standard of living from year to year are the industry norm. Table 4-2 shows the extent to which transit wages outpaced the inflation rate from 1962 through 1973, producing gains in real income for transit workers.

Gains in the real income of wage earners is a trend one would hope to find in an advanced industrial democracy. But in the case of mass transit, the entitlements of labor interact with pressures to maintain a stable fare in a fashion that causes recurrent financial crises. The result is particularly problematic during periods of virulent inflation. We can illustrate how problematic by example.

Suppose that a transit property enters a labor negotiation with a healthy operating ratio of .65. Operating revenues exceed operating costs by a significant margin, and profits will be sizable if the property is conservatively capitalized. Suppose that there is a background inflation rate of 6 percent and a bargaining custom that guarantees that labor's standard of living will improve, but only modestly, from year to year. Let's say that this produces an agreement to increase wages at 7 percent annually, the adjustment necessary to allow labor to better its position by one percentage point relative to the cost of living— hardly an excessive demand. Suppose also that the property is unable to obtain a fare increase or that it wishes to avoid the political confrontation of proposing one and, thus, must continue providing service at a constant fare. *Over a period of just five years*, the property's operating ratio would deteriorate from its healthy basepoint of .65 to .90. It would now be hovering on the verge of receivership. To avoid this outcome, it would be imperative for the property to either seek subsidy or reduce service to shed cost.*

Shedding rush-hour service, the service that occasions the most cost, is pragmatically infeasible. The community's civic and business leadership views the *expansion* of rush-hour service as the *sine qua non* of economic growth. *Reducing* rush-hour service is thus politically unacceptable, and service reductions must be made in the midday or evening hours. The result is that service reductions will produce less than proportionate savings in operating costs because the property's

---

*We have not mentioned expanding service as a strategy to increase net revenues and thus achieve financial recovery. This is because the demand for transit is service inelastic, and increasing service will produce less than a proportionate increase in revenue patronage. Let's say, nevertheless, that the property in our example seeks to improve its financial position by increasing service by, say, 10 percent. The property recognizes that there is no merit in increasing midday service because the service already in place is only lightly patronized. But it does see an opportunity to increase ridership during the rush-hour peak because it seems likely that crowding is discouraging the use of transit for commuting. The property pursues this opportunity and, in fact, realizes the hoped-for increase in ridership, but its financial position is damaged further. This is because a 20 percent increase in *rush-hour* service is necessary to increase *total* service by the targeted 10 percent. The coaches and labor added during the rush-hour must be idled at midday but the property's labor contract requires a full day's pay for what amounts to part-time work. Thus, operating costs increase some 15 percent while service increases by only 10 percent, and assuming a fairly typical service elasticity, revenue patronage increases by only 4 percent. Actual revenues increase by only 3 percent because many of the new patrons use a monthly pass that prices individual trips at a discount rate. Thus, the property's effort to increase net revenues by improving service actually leads to the degradation of its operating ratio from .90 to 1.0. This does not account for the capital cost of adding service in the peak. When interest payments are appropriately considered as an operating cost, the property now operates at a loss and would require tax subsidy to operate at its expanded level of service.

TABLE 4-2 Transit Wages versus Consumer Prices,
1963-1973

Year (July–June)	Actual Wage Increase (%)	CPI Increase (%)	Real Wage Increase (%)
1962–63	3.7%	1.5%	2.8%
1963–64	4.0	1.1	3.6
1964–65	4.2	1.8	2.3
1965–66	4.2	2.7	1.6
1966–67	6.8	2.9	2.3
1967–68	6.6	4.3	1.4
1968–69	7.8	5.5	1.4
1969–70	8.8	5.9	1.5
1970–71	8.5	4.4	1.9
1971–72	6.7	3.0	2.2
1972–73	7.2	5.7	1.3

Source: Mary Kay Rieg, *Monthly Labor Review,* July 1974.
(Washington, D.C.: U.S. Department of Labor)

payroll obligations are dominated by the labor requirements of the peak. Thus the actual economies that can be realized by shedding service are quite limited.

As a result, the property must request public subsidy. This is the only strategy that will allow it to honor its trilateral obligations: (1) its commitment to civic leadership to maintain rush-hour service, (2) its commitment to its riders to maintain essentially constant fares, and (3) its commitment to its work force to increase wages at a rate that will permit modest improvement in their standard of living.

Our scenario of this property's financial dilemma is faithful to the trend of industry performance in all but one regard. Industrywide, transit's decline was more gradual and protracted than we have portrayed. Its dynamic, however, was the same. Transit's decline was more gradual because historical inflation rates were lower than the one used in our scenario and because properties stayed decline by obtaining at least some degree of financial relief through fare increases and by implementing a succession of one-time productivity improvements.

Nevertheless, the scenario we have described accurately portrays the most important dynamic of transit's decline. It also explains transit's continuing financial instability under public ownership. Steadily increasing subsidy is needed to honor transit's trilateral commitment to its work force, its ridership, and the growth establishments of the communities it serves.

Even more subsidy will be required if increased peak-hour service is made a condition of public assistance or is planned as part of a community's strategy of economic growth. And even more subsidy still will be needed if, as a matter of political obligation, service must be extended to suburban markets at the moving margin of the urban periphery. The flat or gently tapered fare structures typical of American transit properties ensure that the farebox ratio of such services will depress the property's average, while the attenuated length of such routes mean that coach and driver may be able to complete only one scheduled run each rush-hour period.

The extension of service to distant suburbs characterized transit development during the 1970s. During this period, transit properties assumed a fourth commitment over and above their traditional obligations to labor, their long-time riders, and the downtown growth establishment: a commitment to provide a basic level of service to communities within the domain of their taxing district, regardless of the market potential or financial results of such operation.[15]

Thus, the politics of vested entitlement go a long way toward explaining why transit has been unable to find a workable strategy of reorganization and renewal, and why financial distress and instability has continued as the industry norm, subsidy notwithstanding. Further explanation can be found in the *compound* character of the change that is needed to match service to markets and slow the escalation of unit labor costs. Incremental change will not suffice, nor will piecemeal adjustment. Compound change in the industry's work rules, wage scales, fleet mix, operating customs, and fare structure is needed, but change of such wrenching proportions is ruled out by the risk of the venture and the politics of vested entitlements.

THE IMPACT OF GENERAL INFLATION

In the previous section, we built a scenario in which the bargaining power of transit workers and the political influence of transit riders combined with general inflation to force a transit property to the brink of receivership and finally into subsidized operation. The pace at which this scenario would be played out is extraordinarily sensitive to the rate at which inflation is increasing the general price level. Table 4-3 shows

TABLE 4-3 Financial Performance Under
Different Inflationary Regimes

	3% Inflation	6% Inflation	9% Inflation
Operating ratio in base year	.65	.65	.65
Operating ratio after five years	.77	.90	1.03[a]

[a] Deficit operation.

the operating ratio that would result for the property in our example under three different inflationary regimes. In each case, the property agrees to a wage increase one percentage point higher than the background inflation rate but is constrained to maintain its fare at a constant level. As the table shows, the *interaction* of vested entitlements with a high rate of inflation is capable of explaining the explosive growth of operating deficits and subsidy requirements that occurred during the 1970s.

Indeed, it allows us to conclude that financial instability continues as the industry norm because special interests have possessed the political influence necessary to protect entitlements vested by history and custom. This is strong language and a controversial conclusion. Let us restate the same proposition more constructively: those with the greatest at stake in the preservation of public transportation have been reluctant to endorse more than incremental changes in the structure of transit service or the framework of the industry's labor contracts. That reluctance is understandable given the risk and difficulty of compound change. But the avoidance of real change should be understood as an implicit choice to accept gradual decline through financial attrition.

Facing what was perceived as a forced choice between public subsidy and eventual extinction, the transit industry sought subsidy—and has required increasing subsidy since.

NOTES

1. Emerson P. Schmidt, *Industrial Relations in Urban Transportation* (Minneapolis: University of Minnesota Press, 1937), pp. 71-74; Edward S. Mason, *The Street Railway in Massachusetts* (Cambridge, Mass.: Harvard University Press, 1932), pp. 114-117.

2. See, for example, Martin Wachs, *Transportation for the Elderly: Changing Lifestyles, Changing Needs* (Berkeley: University of California Press, 1979), p. 66.

3. Richard L. Oram, "The Role of Subsidy Policy in Modernizing the Structure of the Bus Transit Industry," *Transportation* (November 1980), p. 342. See also Arthur Saltzman, "The Decline of Transit," in George Grey and Lester A. Hoel, eds., *Public Transportation: Planning, Operations and Management* (Englewood Cliffs, N.J.: Prentice-Hall, 1979), p. 28.

4. The utilization of equipment in the peak and base period is reported for 60 bus operations in Control Data Corporation, *Trends in Bus Transit Financial and Operating Characteristics, 1960-1975* (Washington, D.C.: U.S. Department of Transportation, 1978), pp. B.29-30. On average, transit properties use twice as many coaches in their peak as in their base schedules.

5. In contracts negotiated by the Amalgamated Transit Union, operators are usually paid $1\frac{1}{2}$ times the base wage for hours worked outside the span of a "normal" workday, defined at 10.8 hours in 1976. For a thorough discussion of work rules and compensation practices, see James L. Stern, et al., *Labor Relations in Urban Transit* (Washington, D.C.: U.S. Department of Transportation, 1977).

6. Charles A. Lave, "Is Part-Time Labor a Cure for Transit Deficits?" *Traffic Quarterly*, January 1980, pp. 61–63.

7. Urban Mass Transportation Administration, *National Urban Mass Transportation Statistics* (Washington, D.C.: U.S. Department of Transportation, 1982), pp. 1–15.

8. American Public Transit Association, *Transit Fact Book, 1981* (Washington, D.C.: APTA, 1981), p. 66.

9. Stern, *Labor Relations in Urban Transit*, p. 177.

10. Transit agencies have little experience with demand-responsive service operated in the central-city environment. Reserved-ride and route-deviation services are primarily a suburban phenomenon or, in central cities, a service provided by social welfare organizations. Requests for such service from social service agencies indicates a significant latent demand for such service in the urban core of transit districts.

11. The postulated reduction in unit costs hinges on (1) the reduction of labor used exclusively in maintenance roles and (2) increased productivity during the off-peak period.

12. U.S. Bureau of the Census, *Electric Railways, 1917* (Washington, D.C.: Government Printing Office, 1920), p. 48.

13. Delos F. Wilcox, *Analysis of the Electric Railway Problem* (published by the author, 1921), pp. 12–14.

14. Ibid., p. 587.

15. David W. Jones, Jr., "The Cost Revenue Squeeze in Conventional Transit Finance," *TRB Special Report No. 184* (Washington, D.C.: Transportation Research Board, 1979), pp. 60–61.

5

THE CASE FOR TRANSIT SUBSIDIES

INTRODUCTION

Subsidy offered a way for transit properties to honor commitments vested by custom and protected by political power: the commitment to maintain and increase peak-hour service in the interest of downtown growth; the commitment to increase wages at a rate that would permit transit workers to realize a modest improvement in their standard of living; and the commitment to riders to maintain essentially constant fares. The political calculus that recommends transit subsidies is an apparent one; subsidy provides the most expedient way in which to avoid confrontation with organized interests and to avert wrenching change in vested entitlements. But subsidy can also be justified on grounds other than expediency. Both economics and English common law provide a social welfare rationale for subsidizing public transportation.

THE ECONOMIC ARGUMENT FOR SUBSIDY

The economic argument for subsidy rests on the work of Margolis and Vickrey, which has demonstrated that public enterprises such as mass transit are unable simultaneously to charge uniform fares, operate without deficit, and produce service of the quantity that would be socially optimal.[1] If transit operations are constrained to break even and charge a uniform fare, less than the optimal level of service can be provided.

Conversely, if the optimal level of service is to be provided at a uniform fare, subsidy will be necessary to pay for the plant and equipment required to serve the peak.

The cost of serving the peak could be recovered if transit could charge so-called "peak-load prices"—fares that are higher during the rush hour than during the midday. But the dilemma of such fares is that they would place transit at a competitive disadvantage relative to the automobile.[2] The automobile used during the rush hour is charged no congestion toll or peak-period surtax. As a result, charging a higher fare for using transit during the rush hour would produce an inefficient allocation of traffic between highways and public transportation. Transit, in short, is unable to price peak-hour service on the basis of true incremental cost because its primary competitor—the highway system—does not do so. Subsidy, then, is necessary to produce an economically efficient division of traffic between highways and mass transit.

THE COMMON LAW RATIONALE FOR SUBSIDY

The traditions of English common law provide a somewhat more philosophical rationale for transit subsidy. Under common law, the provision of transportation service creates rights on the part of those who use and rely on the service provided. To understand the rights created by reliance, it is essential to remember that transportation has no value in and of itself. Its value is attributable to its role as an organizer and facilitator of society's patterns of production, consumption, and leisure. The worth of transportation lies in the opportunity it creates for more efficient production, more extensive distribution, and more selective consumption. In turn, transportation's value depends, in large measure, on the extent to which it can be *relied* on to provide a secure foundation for long-term investment, location, and job-holding decisions.

Once transportation service is introduced and patterns of job holding, household location, business relations, and real estate investment are organized around it, users have a right to expect *reasonable* continuity of service and fares. The Interstate Commerce Commission has enunciated such a doctrine in cases dealing with the commuted fares of suburban rail service. It applies to public transportation in general:

> The prosperity and growth of many communities throughout the country depend upon an efficient and reasonable commutation service. Suburban property has been bought, homes have been established, business relations made, and the entire course of life of many families adjusted to the conditions created by a commutation service. This may not have been done on the theory that the fares in effect at any particular time would always be maintained, but countless homes have been established in suburban communities

in the belief there would be a reasonable continuity in the fares, and that the carriers in any event would perform the service at all times for a reasonable compensation. Suburban communities have grown into existence on the theory, voluntarily accepted by the carriers as well as by the public, that one who makes daily use of an agency of transportation between his place of business and his home must necessarily be accorded a special low rate. This theory is firmly fixed in the history and traditions of transportation by rail.[3]

In short, reasonably stable, but not fixed prices and service levels have the standing of a social contract. This contract obliges government to protect the public from capricious, unpredictable, or precipitous changes in the price or level of transportation services. At the same time, it is unfair, and, in fact, confiscatory, to oblige private carriers to provide services at unremunerative rates. The nexus of these two obligations—to those reliant on service and to those who have invested in transit properties—forms the primary common law argument for subsidizing transit service. Common law argues for subsidy when wrenching change or confiscation present themselves as the only alternatives to subsidy.

The merit of this logic is reinforced when we consider the special case of those who are unable to drive or afford the cost of automobile ownership. As a social group, the transit dependent are among those at the margin of social participation, and the continuation of transit service makes a modest contribution to their ability to live self-reliant lives without debt to friends, relatives, or neighbors for the transportation they need. In this context, it is appropriate for a wealthy society to ensure the continuity of public transportation for those with little or no margin of adaptivity.

This argument suggests that *local* transit subsidy is appropriate. But is federal subsidy appropriate? And is there a *national* interest at stake in the stabilization of *local* transit services? Our answers are "yes." The nation as a whole obtains important financial and governmental services from the corporate headquarters' cities where transit performs functions that are essentially irreplaceable without significant dislocation of economic activity. The pattern of labor market access in many of these centers is dependent on reasonable continuity of transit services and fares—continuity in which the nation as a whole has a stake because hinterland populations benefit from the financial, corporate, and governmental services located in central business districts.

In this context, it can be argued that federal subsidies for transit amount to an administratively efficient proxy for the jigsaw pattern of overlapping benefit tax districts that would have to be assembled to encompass the geographic hinterland of urban centers. The population of those hinterlands benefit indirectly from the public services necessary to support the dense concentration of interdependent economic functions that are the *raison d'être* of big-city central business districts. Thus, federal subsidies can be justified from a tax equity viewpoint. If they remain a relatively small fraction of transit agency operating budgets, federal subsidies serve the function of commensurating tax burdens with service benefits—albeit indirect ones.

In arguing the merits of subsidy, we have been careful to emphasize benefits and obligations to individuals, households, and firms that have a right under common law to expect reasonable continuity of service and fares. The providers of transportation have no comparable right to expect stable markets or stable earnings without risk. Thus, it is not appropriate to ask that public policy protect inefficient organizations from the vicissitudes of market change or economic obsolescence. In fact, policy should reward carriers that adapt to changing preferences, changing travel patterns, and new technological opportunities. Subsidy, simply put, should not reward inefficiency or shelter incompetence.

It is also inappropriate for subsidy to serve as the budget balancer that increases whenever it is necessary to fill the gap between rising costs and fixed fares—a formula for endlessly increasing subsidy and the abuse of the general taxpayer. The taxpayer is a party at interest in the subsidy of public transportation, and the social contract that leads to subsidy should protect the taxpayer from open-ended tax obligations. In fact, the rights of taxpayers are as important as the rights of those reliant on a reasonable continuity of service and fares, and subsidy can be justified only if it is based on a social contract that protects the interests of both users and taxpayers.

As we have just seen, common law offers what amounts to a social contract theory for the justification for transit subsidy. Subsidy can be justified because it preserves a social contract with those who have relied on the continuity of service in making decisions about location, job holding, and long-term investment. But subsidy cannot be justified if its consequence is to shelter inefficiency or shift the burden of exponentiating costs to the taxpayer at large. This means that the merits of subsidy hinge on the design of the subsidy program. Transit subsidy has merit if it can simultaneously

Protect users from unreasonable or precipitous change in the level of fares or service

Protect private carriers from the confiscation that would result if service had to be operated on an unremunerative basis

Protect taxpayers from obligations that increase steadily due to a widening gap between costs and revenues

Reward efforts to increase the efficiency and responsiveness of operation.

Subsidy does not have merit if it is *only* an expedient way for transit properties to honor commitments vested by custom and perpetuated by dint of political influence. A subsidy program based on expediency would most probably invite inefficiency and impose increasingly burdensome obligations on the general taxpayer.

Economists who advocate transit subsidies share this concern, namely, that the provision of subsidies is as likely to encourage waste and inefficiency as it is to produce output of optimal quantity.[4] These economists would agree that the merits of subsidy hinge on the art of program design, and many would question whether the political process is capable of the disciplined craftsmanship necessary to devise a program of appropriate design.

As we shall see, there is good reason for such concern. The next chapter will show that the subsidy program that Congress devised in the 1960s and 1970s was, in large measure, a product of political expediency. It was premised on a faulty diagnosis of the dynamics of transit's distress; it shied from structural change; and it vested new entitlements to new services that are arguably unwarranted.

NOTES

1. See Julius Margolis, "Welfare Criteria, Pricing and Decentralization of a Public Service," *Quarterly Journal of Economics*, Vol. 71 (August 1957), pp. 449-453; William S. Vickrey, "Economic Efficiency and Pricing," in Selma Mushkin, ed., *Public Prices for Public Products* (Washington, D.C.: The Brookings Institute, 1972), pp. 67-70. See also Matthew Edel, *Economics and the Environment* (Englewood Cliffs, N.J.: Prentice-Hall, 1973), pp. 120-123, and Tillo E. Kuhn, *Public Enterprise Economics and Transport Problems* (Berkeley: University of California Press, 1962), pp. 143-145.

2. Vickrey, "Efficiency and Pricing," p. 68.

3. *Commutation Fares*, 33 ICC 428, 435 (1915). For discussion see Emery Troxel, *Economics of Transport* (New York: Rinehart & Co., 1955), p. 760; Charles H. Freed, *The Story of Railroad Passenger Fares* (Washington, D.C.: by the author, 1942), pp. 233-240.

4. See, for example, Leonard Merewitz, *Impacts of the Urban Mass Transportation Administration Capital Grants Program* (Washington, D.C.: National Transportation Policy Study Commission, 1979), pp. 20-23; Jose A. Gomez-Ibanez, "Assessing the Arguments for Urban Transit Operating Subsidies," in Herbert S. Levinson and Robert A. Weant, eds., *Urban Transportation—Perspectives and Prospects* (Westport, Conn.: ENO Foundation for Transportation, 1982), pp. 131-132.

6

THE POLITICS OF FEDERAL SUBSIDY

INTRODUCTION

The legislative history of federal aid for mass transit is a study in persistent advocacy and artful coalition building.[1] It required extra-ordinary political craftsmanship to secure first a favorable hearing and then a majority vote for transit aid. But the legislative history of the transit aid program is also a study in the exigencies of congressional politics and the way in which they can compromise program design and prejudice program outcomes.

As we shall see, the impetus for federal subsidy came from rail-roads and the mayors of the few cities served by railroad commuter service. The urban transit properties that are the workhorses of the industry joined the federal aid coalition after its agenda had been shaped and fixed.[2] Thus, the structure and thrust of the federal aid pro-gram was only obliquely responsive to the problems of city properties; it addressed their symptomatic need for financial relief without attack-ing the underlying causes of their financial distress.

We shall also see how the federal transit program developed its bias toward capital-intensive rail transit systems of the type represented by BART and the Washington Metro. Such systems dominated the invest-ment portfolio of the federal aid program through the 1960s and 1970s, accounting for 76 percent of federal outlays from 1965 to 1970.[3]

THE ORIGINS OF FEDERAL INVOLVEMENT

Congressional attention was first focused on the problems of urban commuting by events that followed the enactment of the Transportation Act of 1958. The 1958 Act included a provision that allowed railroads to reduce or abandon commuter services if it could be shown that passenger losses were imposing a financial burden on other railroad operations.[4] The legislation gave railroads an opportunity to seek Interstate Commerce Commission relief when state regulatory agencies denied petitions for the abandonment of intrastate commuter services. And it adopted a permissive standard for abandoning commuter services operated across state lines.

The 1958 legislation triggered a mild round of abandonments in the Midatlantic States and allowed railroads to posture that deep-cutting service reduction would follow unless state subsidies were forthcoming. In New York and New Jersey, arrangements for state aid were negotiated, and most commuter service was preserved on the new subsidized basis.

In Philadelphia, railroad leadership negotiated for *city* assistance, tapping uncommitted funds in the federally funded Model Cities budget. Model Cities funding for the Pennsylvania Railroad was a temporary arrangement, but one with long-range consequences. It led Philadelphia Mayor Richardson Dilworth and Pennsylvania Railroad Company Chairman James Symes to agreement that federal aid for commuter service was both needed and appropriate, a significant break with the traditional position of the railroad industry.

The Symes/Dilworth–City/Railroad alliance was the cornerstone of what was to become the transit aid lobby. That lobby took form when Symes and Dilworth convened a meeting of urban mayors and railroad presidents in early 1959.[5] The mayors and railroad executives agreed to lobby for federal aid, drafting a resolution that was to shape and focus the thrust of federal transit policy in future years:

Metropolitan areas are gaining in population at an ever accelerating rate. By 1980 more than 80% of the nation's people will live in some 160 great urban areas. Neither highways nor aviation can meet the transportation needs of these people. Not only would the cost be prohibitive, the amount of land required for highways and parking facilities would take so much of the usable space in any urban area as to defeat its own purpose. The metropolitan areas cannot be the healthy backbones of the urban civilization already upon us, unless people can move freely within and through these areas.

Therefore, it is apparent that high-speed mass transportation, particularly in the form of rail, both surface and subway, must play a vital, important part in furnishing transportation to the great urban areas. Unless constructive measures are taken immediately, nearly all urban areas are in danger of actually losing their commuter railroad facilities. It is clear to the railroads and to the cities that means must be found immediately to keep this from happening.

Neither the cities nor the railroads can finance such a program by themselves. We believe that four steps should be taken immediately by the Congress of the United States toward the solution of this problem which is so vital to the nation as a whole:

1. That a national policy should be established by the Congress for a balanced and coordinated transportation system.
2. That the Federal, state and local governments be asked to develop rational tax policies for the railroads.
3. That Federal loans be made available where necessary to municipalities or publicly constituted bodies for new commuter equipment and improved facilities and for the improvement of intracity mass passenger transportation facilities; these to be long term, low interest loans.
4. That a study be made of grants-in-aid by the Federal Government to communities or duly constituted public bodies which have a sound plan for the permanent improvement of commutation or other intracity transportation facilities, this to be modeled on the present urban renewal program.[6]

Twelve mayors and 17 railroad executives were involved in the initial meeting that led to the resolution to seek federal aid. Their respective membership in the American Municipal Association and the Executive Committee of the American Association of Railroads led both associations to endorse the resolution within months.

Thus, it would be the Philadelphia model—*federal* capital grants—and not the New Jersey model—*state* purchase-of-service contracts—that became the primary legislative objective of railroads and big-city mayors. It is not exaggerating to say that the agenda of the original proponents of federal aid was determined as much by accidental precedent as by design. The policy they advocated was based on the "Philadelphia precedent," and its thrust was established without involvement of the *urban* transit properties that are the workhorses of the public transportation industry.

The urban rail coalition's first overtures for federal assistance for commuter railroads were rebuffed in the public works committees of Congress, committees attuned to the priority of highway spending. A tactical decision followed: to seek hearings from a committee more responsive to urban concerns.[7] Thus, the proponents of federal aid framed draft legislation so that it fell within the jurisdiction of the committee responsible for urban renewal—the Housing Subcommittee of the Senate Banking, Currency and Urban Affairs Committee.

This tactical decision had significant strategic consequences. It meant that federal aid for transit would be divorced from the federal-state-local pipeline of the highway program and that the Model Cities/urban renewal precedent of federal-city partnership would be the organizational model on which the program eventually would be based. Thus the tactical requirements of obtaining a receptive hearing dictated that transit aid be sought within the framework of federal aid for urban renewal rather than federal aid for transportation.

The heavy investment that the transit program would eventually make in rail rapid transit and the lack of enthusiasm for bus-on-freeway transit is understandable in this context because the construction of rail systems was seen as an important strategy of urban renewal by city planners in the orbit of redevelopment agencies. It is unlikely that the transit aid program would have developed such a heavy bias toward rail transit if it had been configured as a formula grant program and managed as an element of federal-state-local partnership of the highway program—if only because formula apportionments would not have permitted the concentration of investment necessary to finance rail rapid transit projects.

The tradition of active mayoral involvement in urban renewal grantsmanship would also influence the transit aid program, imparting a further bias toward high-visibility, high-technology projects. Rapid transit is a politically imageable technology; buses are far less so. Mayoral involvement in transit grantsmanship would also influence the program in another way—immersing it in the reward and punishment games of presidential election-year politics.

Assignment of transit finance matters to the Senate Banking, Currency and Urban Affairs Committee provided the opportunity for Senator Harrison Williams to assume a role as the program's leading advocate. Political scientist Michael Danielson explains Williams's emergence as the program's champion:

> A compound of personal interest, ambition, and opportunity, conditioned, of course, by the broader context of his metropolitan background and generalized constituency concern, led him to make a bid for leadership on the federal aid aspect of the commuter issue. Such a move also fitted in with a notion developing in the mind of the Senator and his aids that Williams, representing the nation's most urbanized state, had a golden opportunity to enhance his position by specializing in metropolitan problems, up to this time a neglected area of congressional concern. Williams already had taken a step in this direction by obtaining a place on the Banking and Currency Committee's Housing Subcommittee, the natural focus of a great deal of the Senate's urban activities.[8]

Williams proceeded to craft legislation that would attract the broadest possible congressional constituency.[9] He did so by:

Broadening the program's thrust to provide for public transit in general, rather than commuter railroads in particular

Limiting federal assistance to low-interest loans, a strategy designed to avoid the perception that the federal government would be "subsidizing" private enterprise or providing regular assistance over a sustained period

Seeking a relatively small initial authorization: $100 million.

Williams's approach blunted opposition to federal involvement in "a matter of purely local concern" and deflected criticism that the program was special interest legislation instigated at the behest of a few Eastern railroads. It also created the imagery that a relatively small federal commitment would provide the transfusion necessary to restore the transit industry to a competitive footing. The magnitude of assistance proposed also blunted opposition to federal involvement—although concern about "opening Pandora's box" was voiced during the congressional debate.

Danielson describes the stage management of the hearing process as follows:

> The main sources of support for positive federal involvement came from central-city political leaders and the Eastern commuter railroads. In 1960, planners, metropolitan transportation experts, and urban specialists from the academic community were added to the ranks. The following year, increased publicity and the efforts of Williams, Dilworth, Wagner, Symes, and Alpert brought the transit industry, central-city business interests, and the metropolitan press aboard the bandwagon. By the spring of 1961, the federal mass transportation coalition bore a close resemblance to the familiar urban alliance of "downtown stores, real estate interests concerned with central city property values, commuter railways, central city banks, central city and other politicians concerned with the implications of the worsening of the central city tax base," making "common cause with the press, university professors, the foundations and the civic leaders in a crusade to save downtown."

> Williams sought to impress Congress with the national impact of the mass transportation problem by inviting witnesses from outside the large Eastern metropolitan centers. He was particularly eager to avoid a preponderance of participants from the New York region. And to broaden his base of support in Congress, Williams wanted the hearings to draw attention to all aspects of the mass transportation problem, rather than just the woes of the commuter railroads. Yet this careful planning could not disguise the fact that support for the bill was concentrated almost exclusively in the central cities of the large metropolitan areas.

> Williams' striving for geographical balance was reflected in the presence for the first time at a federal mass transportation assistance conclave of represen-

tatives from the West Coast. The presence of the heads of the proposed Los Angeles and San Francisco rapid transit systems, as well as of the chairman of the Chicago Transit Authority, indicated the broadening of the base of support for federal aid beyond its commuter rail origins. Even New York City, which had originally geared its approach to federal assistance on a commuter railroad rationale, now was talking in terms of federal aid for the city subway system.[10]

Danielson's interpretation accurately reflects the limited role that old-line urban transit properties played in the drive for federal aid. As Danielson's analysis suggests, urban officials did not perceive the need for federal subsidies for city transit systems until a congressional consensus favoring subsidy was virtually in place. Williams himself made little effort to establish a factual basis for the claim that cities did not have sufficient revenues to subsidize local transit services. Instead, Williams argued that federal funds were necessary to *motivate* localities to address a problem they had heretofore neglected. The senator told his colleagues that federal aid would "encourage the involvement and participation of State and local governments to come to grips with the problem—financially and otherwise."[11]

Political histories such as Danielson's have focused on the artfulness with which transit champions assembled a broad-based coalition to support federal aid. From its commuter railroad origins, the federal aid constituency was broadened steadily to a metropolitan coalition and later included the advocates of transit services for the rural poor. Written by political scientists, these histories have not been concerned with the way in which the requirements of coalition building affected the design, thrust, and effectiveness of policy. We will focus on these neglected dimensions of legislative history, emphasizing the way in which consensus politics influenced the thrust of the program that was eventually adopted.

THE SHAPE OF CONGRESSIONAL POLICY

The 1960 and 1961 hearings orchestrated by Senator Williams imprinted what would become the Urban Mass Transportation Assistance Program with (1) a particular interpretation of "the metropolitan transportation problem," (2) a particular interpretation of the decline of mass transit, and (3) a particular view of the strategy necessary to "preserve and improve mass transportation" and stimulate "self-recovery."[12] The hearings also broached a menu of technical measures thought appropriate to implement that strategy. We will examine each in turn.

The Shape of the Problem

Senator Williams and the witnesses before his committee focused congressional attention on the population growth of metropolitan areas and corresponding increases in urban auto use.[13] The trend of population growth was characterized as explosive and the trend of traffic growth as strangling. Virtually no emphasis was placed on the decline of central-city resident population that had occurred during the previous decade in virtually all the nation's major transit markets or its implications for the economic base of the transit industry. When changes in the geographic pattern of travel and the structure of metropolitan employment location *were* noted, they were discussed normatively as *undesirable* trends rather than as problematic factors that should influence program design. Thus, the program was cast as a response to the problems of traffic and population growth rather than the problems of a distressed industry in a declining market. In turn, this interpretation of the urban transportation problem led to a transit policy that was focused by the narrow concern that the industry have access to sufficient capital to expand capacity at the pace of metropolitan growth.

Interpreting Transit's Decline

Virtually no effort was made to diagnose and explain the dynamics of transit's declining patronage and impaired earning power. Nevertheless, the committee hearing record and the federal aid program the committee shaped are imprinted with an *implicit* theory explaining the "serious financial and physical decline in mass transportation service" and "the gap of rising costs and declining revenues facing our private carriers, which is forcing them necessarily and inevitably to prune, curtail, and abandon service whenever possible."[14]

The theory of transit's decline implicit in the legislation emphasized the loss of patronage due to the sorry condition of the industry's physical plant. The inability of private carriers to attract capital investment for the modernization and extension of service was seen as a consequence of the imbalance of federal policy and its bias toward freeway construction. It was also interpreted as a consequence of the failure of localities to manage urban development and coordinate highway, transit, and land-use planning. This, in turn, was seen as a by-product of the fragmentation of governmental responsibilities in metropolitan areas.[15]

Virtually no attention was given to the economics of transit operations. Only passing notice was given to the impact of state regulatory policies on transit's effective earning power.[16] Little attention was given to the operating costs that would be associated with expanding peak-hour transit services as Senator Williams was to propose. Nor was much attention given to fundamental changes in life-styles that were altering the spatial arrangements of metropolitan areas, the geography of trip making, and temporal rhythms of transit's residual traffic.

It is not just thanks to the advantage of hindsight that we know to raise these issues neglected in the Williams hearings. Issues that the Housing Subcommittee gave short shrift had, for decades, been *central* concerns of urban transit properties and their trade association, the American Transit Association (ATA). Thus, it is interesting to note that few urban properties were represented at the early congressional hearings that shaped the thrust of the federal aid program.

It is also interesting to note that the 1961 testimony of the ATA was, in fact, jarringly dissonant with the world view represented by witnesses with a railroad or rapid transit orientation.[17] The ATA's testimony emphasized problems of coordination with traffic and highway engineering agencies—problems of street and highway design and operation. It also focused on problems of fare policy and earning power in a regulated environment. These issues did not square with the agenda for which Senator Williams was building support and were pushed aside in the process of policy design. Thus, the hearing record reveals the extraordinary degree to which federal policy was being constructed in terms of the world view of the suburbs-to-central-city commuter. Even though transit properties that operate in mixed traffic are the workhorses of the industry, the problems intrinsic to urban street operations were not congruent with the committee's world view and did not inform the policy it formulated. Indeed, policy was being built for and around the racehorses, not the workhorses, of the transit industry.

The Strategic Thrust of Policy

The political consensus engineered by Senator Williams and the urban rail alliance gave federal transit policy its thrust and direction for its first 20 years. At the heart of that thrust was

1. An endorsement of the merits of rail transit and, by implication, grants-in-aid for very-large-scale capital investment
2. A commitment to capitalize transit development in urban areas of all sizes—including both the rehabilitation of older transit systems and the deployment of new ones
3. A commitment to a direct city-federal partnership without state involvement in the transit funding pipeline
4. A commitment that aid to private transit properties and com-

muter railroads would be funneled through institutions of local government

5. A faith in the development-shaping, growth-inducing impacts of rail transit systems

Thus, the strategy of transit development that Congress embraced was fashioned in the image of the Philadelphia/Pennsylvania Railroad collaboration in the East and the development of BART in San Francisco, the two "success stories" showcased in the Williams hearings. Both, of course, were rail-centered models of transit improvement.

The Tactical Thrust of Policy

Always attentive to the geographic and modal balance of the program, Senator Williams embraced a broad menu of tactical measures studiously composed to improve transit service in both large and small urban areas. Senator Williams itemized 15 "major elements" he viewed as the appropriate project content of a transit development program:

1. Modernization of rail commuter cars and equipment
2. Relocation or extension or coordination of rail commuter track, stations, or terminals
3. Improvement of rail commuter service frequency and lowering of fares
4. Conversion of rail commuter service to rapid transit–type operation and utilization of unused freight trackage
5. Construction of new or expansion of existing rail rapid transit, either underground, surface, or elevated
6. Coordination of rail commuter service with rapid transit for interchangeable use
7. Provision of express bus service and reserved bus lanes on highways and major arteries
8. Extension of bus service to presently unprofitable low-density suburban areas
9. Improvement of bus service frequency and lower fares
10. Provision of better bus feeder and transfer service to commuter rail or rapid transit terminals and stations, including coordination of schedules
11. Provision of fringe area parking adjacent to express bus, commuter rail, or rapid transit lines
12. Coordination among mass transportation facilities and coordination of mass transportation facilities with new highway networks

13. Lower taxi fares and development in downtown areas of "carveyors" or similar systems

14. Incorporation of feasible new technological developments into all modes of mass transportation wherever and whenever possible

15. Coordination of mass transportation facilities with housing, urban renewal, and other land-use developments.[18]

At first glance, the portfolio of projects proposed by Williams appears both remarkably balanced and comprehensive—as it was intended to be. It was, in fact, endorsed by later administrators of the federal aid program and embraced in the 1960s and 1970s as a balanced strategy of transit recovery—one designed to increase ridership, enhance transit's competitive position relative to the automobile, and increase transit's share of the critical commuter market, thus reducing congestion and its adverse impacts on downtown economies.

The dilemma with the strategy Congress embraced is that most of its elements were guaranteed to increase operating costs, aggravate operating deficits, and reduce the industry's productivity. At the time Congress considered the Williams bill, it is doubtful that these impacts or the eventual cost of the program were anticipated, although the chairman of the Pennsylvania Railroad candidly characterized low-interest loans as "a gate opener to an intelligent attack on the problem."[19] Senator Williams predicted that loan guarantees would "lead to major efforts at self-recovery by the local public and private institutions, enabling them to go the rest of the way alone" and that it would "help considerably to reverse the trend toward discontinuing, curtailing and abandoning vital rail, transit and bus service."[20] But he also warned that "It may well be that the experience acquired under this legislation will find the problems more intractable and the need for Federal leadership and assistance much greater."[21]

At any rate, the Williams hearings and the crafting of legislation that required a minimum financial commitment allowed the urban-rail alliance to begin mustering floor support for the loan program and demonstration project funds.

Enactment

Calculating that Williams had assembled majority support for federal aid, the Kennedy administration reluctantly supported the legislation.[22] In exchange for a further reduction in the already small appropriation sought, the administration also agreed to an assessment of transit needs and a study of the appropriate form of long-term federal involvement in urban transportation. With administration support, the first transit aid bill was passed by Congress and signed into law on

June 30, 1961. It authorized $50 million in low-interest loans and $25 million for demonstration projects.

With this opening wedge established, transit lobbyists began marshalling support for an urban renewal–style capital grant program that, as Danielson notes, "had always been the ultimate objective of the urban-rail alliance."[23]

The study of transit needs commissioned in 1961 was reported to Congress in 1962. It recommended a sustained program of capital grants to be distributed at the discretion of federal transit officials. The study was conducted by the Institute of Public Administration, a New York–based think tank committed to the concept of comprehensive regional planning at the metropolitan scale. IPA's diagnosis of the "urban transportation problem" and its prescription emphasized the institutional dimension of transit development:

> Institutional weaknesses underlie the failure of most public programs to date to produce larger and lasting improvements in urban transportation systems. . . . Present fragmentation of planning and administration of urban transportation along modal and jurisdictional lines precludes consideration of metropolitan transportation as an integral and open system. . . . Federal assistance for urban mass transportation improvement should be predicated on comprehensive regional transportation plans integrated with over-all regional plans. The first concern should be with organization and planning rather than with transportation projects per se.[24]

The IPA report reinforced the perception that comprehensive planning combined with a relatively small infusion of federal aid would restore transit to a competitive footing.[25]

As did the Williams hearings, the IPA study had an important influence on the way in which transit issues were perceived in Congress and consequently left an important imprint on the program's design and administration. The IPA report reinforced the view that transit's financial distress is a recent phenomenon—a product of the postwar period. It attributed transit's decline in roughly equal measure to

1. The competitive disadvantage created by federal aid for urban freeways and expressways
2. The failure to coordinate transportation and land-use development so as to create patterns of urbanization compatible with public transportation
3. The physical deterioration of transit facilities and the failure to modernize aging fleets.

As did the testimony before the Williams subcommittee, this interpretation of transit's distress suggests that revitalization could be accomplished without significant changes in the structure of the industry. It also suggests that a one-time infusion of federal assistance combined with authoritative regional development planning could restore the industry to a stable competitive footing.

The IPA also stressed that some forms of mass transit—rapid transit, in particular—had performed better than had the industry in general. This was attributed to inherently superior service attributes—to the intrinsic technological superiority of rapid transit operated on exclusive rights-of-way.

The IPA also ventured an estimate of "transit needs"—an estimate that reinforced the view that a relatively small program of transitional assistance was sufficient to reequip the industry and restore it to a competitive position. IPA's $5 billion estimate was to serve as a benchmark for later congressional debate, although in reality, the IPA estimate of "need" was little more than a tally of local ambitions in cities considering new rapid transit systems.[26] Congress was provided with no estimate of the cost of rehabilitating the worn-out infrastructure of established rail and bus systems in the older transit-dependent cities of the frostbelt, although these were precisely the operations characterized as the most essential transit services in the IPA's report to Congress.

From the IPA's vantage point, the most important element of transit development policy was the creation of the institutional machinery necessary for regional planning at the metropolitan scale.[27] Thus, the report emphasized *developmental planning* for new systems to accommodate future growth rather than a *stabilization policy* designed to rehabilitate and reorganize established properties in declining markets.

The IPA's emphasis on comprehensive regional development planning had important influence on the eventual shape of the UMTA program. It led to the conclusion that federal aid should take the form of a discretionary grant program so that UMTA could leverage the creation of regional planning agencies by conditioning grant approval on the development of authoritative metropolitan development plans. It also led to the conclusion that the link between transportation and land-use planning was more important than was the link between transit operation and street and highway engineering.

IPA's conception of the appropriate thrust of a federal aid program reinforced the view that transit could be an effective instrument of urban renewal and areawide development. It also laid the conceptual groundwork for a program that would become heavily committed to the construction of rail transit systems and organizationally independent from the locus of highway and traffic engineering activities in state and local government. IPA's emphasis on regional planning also served to distance transit development from the zoning and permit activities of municipal governments.

The transit lobby and HUD's transit bureau rallied around the IPA report and marshalled congressional support for the capital grants it recommended, and a modest program of capital grants was authorized in 1964.

THE EXPANSION OF FEDERAL INVOLVEMENT

The transit coalition was broadened by the events of the mid- and late 1960s: ghetto riots, the Vietnam war, the emergence of organized opposition to urban freeway construction, and the growth of environmentalism.[28] The common thread of these events was the grass-roots activism they generated.

During the 1960s, civil rights and antiwar activists, community organizers, conservationists restyled as environmentalists, public interest law groups, and intellectuals of the New Left emerged as a loosely organized coalition with overlapping memberships. The coalition styled itself "The Movement" and found common cause in opposition to what might be called the "growth establishment," namely, the financial institutions, development interests, resource corporations, and commerce associations that exhibited an exploitative interest in suburban growth and bulldozer-style urban renewal. This opposition extended to government agencies with an organizational interest in urban highway projects, bulldozer renewal, and "growth for its own sake."

The Movement embraced mass transit and vested it with new importance based on new imperatives:

1. It would rescue cities from the automobile and freeway construction.
2. It would reduce air pollution.
3. It would conserve land.
4. It would reemploy the workers of the military-industrial complex in the development of peacetime technology.

Not all these claims for transit were new, but they were expressed with new force through their association with the organizing themes of The Movement—the fight against reckless growth, corporate exploitation, and neighborhood powerlessness.

Movement rhetoric was never compelling to the broad spectrum of the American public, but local activism did command media attention, focusing broad public attention on automotive pollution, the disruption of neighborhoods by freeway construction, the loss of urban open space, and the loss of neighborhood amenity. Media attention to environmental issues generated broad support for mass transit development and automotive pollution control, with the two policies frequently paired in media accounts.[29] Most important, *support for transit was established as a litmus test of the environmental credentials of elected officials*, and congressional support for additional federal aid grew in bandwagon fashion.

Senator Williams and the urban-rail alliance pressed their advantage and proposed a significant augmentation of the capital grant program. As a result, federal outlays for transit increased from $281 million in fiscal year 1970 to $517 million in fiscal year 1971.[30]

It is worth noting at this point how the augmented program squared with the financial "needs" of local transit operations. By 1970, the conversion of the more important transit properties from private to public ownership was virtually complete, and the replacement of aging bus fleets was proceeding apace.[31]

Operating funds and the industry's obsolescent structure, not a shortage of capital, were the bottlenecks constraining service expansion. In this context, budget augmentation for *capital investment* amounted to a commitment to rail systems—the only projects costly enough to absorb such a large infusion of funds restricted to capital investment purposes. A more balanced program of capital grants, operating assistance, and structural change would have produced a rather different portfolio of projects from those planned in the early 1970s. As it was configured, the program encouraged even relatively small communities with thin transit markets to initiate planning for fixed guideway systems.

Encouraged by congressional action on mass transit, air quality, and water pollution, Movement activists launched a campaign to free highway trust fund revenues for transit development.[32] The bedrock transit lobby—the downtown/commuter railroad alliance—demurred, preferring to avoid a direct confrontation with highway construction interests. But Movement activists were not deterred. They rallied an Environmental Action Coalition for a sustained two-year lobbying campaign to "Bust the Trust." Activists who had organized antiwar demonstrations and bitterly opposed the Nixon administration's Vietnam policy found support within the same administration for the concept of a Unified Transportation Fund. The Department of Transportation endorsed flexible use of highway funds as a companion measure to general revenue sharing and part of its broader effort to return budget decisions to local control. The confluence of activist support for transit and Republican support for defederalization led to congressional approval of the Federal Aid Highway Act of 1973. The act raised the matching share for transit projects to 80 percent, that is, approximate parity with the federal contribution for highways—and it allowed urban areas to exchange earmarked interstate highway construction funds for an equal entitlement of transit capital assistance. Cities that have invoked the interstate transfer provision are planning rail systems rather than bus acquisition. Because the sums generated by interstate transfers are large and can only be used for *capital* investment, a bus purchase of such magnitude would require a correspondingly massive local commitment to operating subsidies. Rail systems are better suited to drawing down a locality's full transfer entitlement without obligating as large amounts for future operating expenses. Thus, the 1973 Highway Act compounded the effect of the 1970 transit aid bill, reinforcing the bias of transit development toward capital-intensive guideway systems.

The increasingly evident bias of the federal transit program toward rail systems persuaded the Ford administration to endorse federal operating subsidies for mass transit.[33] Traditional congressional reluctance to endorse a continuing budget obligation for operating expenses was overwhelmed by the Arab oil embargo of 1973 and its disruption of auto travel. Despite the crisis mood generated by the embargo and gas lines, majority support for operating subsidies hinged on the geographic balance of the program. Senator Williams and the commuter rail coalition advocated subsidies keyed to the level of service provided; the administration sought to configure a program that would reward the introduction of new service; and the congressional majority balked at both approaches.[34] The House fashioned a bill based on the principle of geographic parity, tempered by a weighting for population density. The compromise bill apportioned operating subsidies on the basis of population and population density. In terms of per capita expenditures, the formula favored the densely settled, transit-dependent cities of the frostbelt. But in terms of subsidy per transit rider, a more germane measure of distributive effect, the formula favored transit riders in smaller cities.

The federal operating assistance authorized in 1974 did little to ease the budget pressures on the large transit systems of the industrial Northeast and Midwest. Federal aid represented only a small proportion of the operating budgets of the largest and oldest transit systems, an amount roughly equivalent to a year's respite from the impacts of inflation on operating deficits.[35]

The apparent shortcomings of the 1974 formula, particularly its failure to target revenues where transit's financial distress was most severe, led to legislative revision in 1978. The formula approved in 1978 added a special tier of operating assistance based on the coach miles of rail service provided.

In 1980, Congress considered, but then tabled, legislation that would have apportioned operating subsidies on the basis of transit ridership. Such a measure would have targeted operating subsidies in markets with an established transit riding habit, rewarding localities that have made the largest financial commitments to transit over time.

FROM EXPANSION TO AMBIVALENCE

The 1980 election marked a turning point in the expansionist path of federal aid for transit. In its first year in office, the Reagan administration proposed the elimination of federal operating subsidies for transit and the reduction of capital grant outlays by a cumulative $4.6 billion over a six-year budget period.[36] It proposed to continue federal spending for bus replacement, bus acquisition, and rail modernization, but it signaled that grants for development of new rail systems modeled on the BART prototype would no longer be forthcoming.

The Reagan proposal was based on the following assessment of program performance:

> The construction of new rail transit systems or extensions has not proved to be as cost-effective as less capital-intensive projects.

> [Rapid] transit system energy savings are . . . [too] small in the short run and too speculative in the long run to justify major Federal investment on energy efficiency grounds.

> Federal operating subsidies "often support marginally effective conventional transit services and prevent transportation needs from being served by more cost-effective alternatives such as carpools, vanpools, subscription bus, and jitney services."

> Transit operating subsidies for everyone—rich and poor alike—are a terribly inefficient way to assist particular disadvantaged groups such as the elderly, the poor, minorities, and youth.[37]

Perhaps, more important, budget officials in the Reagan administration concluded that federal involvement itself—the availability of federal funds—has led to inefficient transit development. This conclusion explains why the Reagan leadership sought to retreat from active federal involvement as opposed to restructuring the thrust of the federal aid program.

In the chapters that follow, we will examine the merits of the federal subsidy program—and the merits of the argument that federal involvement has led to the perpetuation and expansion of inefficient service. As have the officials of the Reagan administration, we will argue that federal aid has not fostered the basic changes in form and function necessary to restore transit to a more stable, competitive footing. But we will take that argument to a different conclusion—one that endorses active federal involvement in the improvement of transit productivity.

NOTES

1. Michael N. Danielson, *Federal-Metropolitan Politics and the Commuter Crisis* (New York: Columbia University Press, 1965), pp. 160-179.

2. Ibid., p. 140.

3. U.S. Department of Transportation, Office of the Assistant Secretary for Policy and International Affairs, *Federal Transportation Financial Statistics, 1970-1979* (Washington, D.C.: U.S. Department of Transportation, 1980), p. S-1.

4. Danielson, *Federal-Metropolitan Politics*, pp. 34-35.

5. Ibid., p. 101.

6. Reproduced in *Hearings on S. 345*, Subcommittee on Housing, Senate Committee on Banking and Currency (Washington, D.C.: Government Printing Office, 1961), pp. 78-79.

7. Danielson, *Federal-Metropolitan Politics*, pp. 110-113.

8. Ibid., pp. 130-131.

9. Ibid., p. 132.

10. Ibid., pp. 138-139.

11. *Hearings on S. 345*, Senate Banking Committee, p. 36.

12. Ibid., p. 36.

13. Ibid., pp. 26-27.

14. Ibid., p. 28.

15. Ibid., pp. 32-33, 204-206.

16. Ibid., p. 374.

17. Ibid., pp. 371-378.

18. Ibid., pp. 29-30.

19. *Hearings on S. 345*, Senate Banking Committee, p. 180.

20. Ibid., p. 26.

21. Ibid.

22. Ibid., p. 157.

23. Ibid., p. 175.

24. Lyle C. Fitch, *Urban Transportation and Public Policy* (San Francisco: Chandler, 1964), pp. 7, 15-16.

25. Ibid., p. 8.

26. Committee on Banking and Currency, U.S. House of Representatives, *Hearings on H.R. 11158* (Washington, D.C.: Government Printing Office, 1962), p. 46.

27. Fitch, *Urban Transportation*, pp. 7, 245.

28. The author was a participant in the so-called "new politics" of the 1960s. The observations that follow are based on personal experience.

29. David W. Jones, Jr., *The Press and the Politics of Urban Growth* (Unpublished Ph.D. thesis, Stanford University, Stanford, Calif., 1974), p. 176.

30. U.S. Department of Transportation, Office of the Assistant Secretary for Policy and International Affairs, *Trends in Federal Transportation Financial Activity* (Washington, D.C.: U.S. Department of Transportation, 1980), p. B-1.

31. Properties accounting for 77 percent of the nation's transit ridership were publicly owned by 1970 according to the American Public Transit Association, *Fact Book 1981*.

32. David W. Jones, Jr. and James F. Miller, Jr., "The Congressional Politics of Transportation Expenditure," in *A Technology Assessment of Future Intercity Passenger Transportation Systems* (National Aeronautics and Space Administration, 1976), pp. IV-20-26.

33. Michael J. Malbin, "Mass Transit Bills Slowed by Jurisdictional Dispute," *National Journal Reports*, April 20, 1974, p. 576. See also Arthur J. Magida, "Transit Lobby Charts Post-Recess Campaign for Subsidies," *National Journal Reports*, November 9, 1974, p. 1688.

34. Malbin, "Mass Transit Bills," p. 574.

35. Urban Mass Transportation Administration, *National Urban Mass Transportation Statistics* (Washington, D.C.: U.S. Department of Transportation, 1982), pp. 2.17-2.18.

36. *America's New Beginning: A Program for Economic Recovery* (Washington, D.C.: The White House, 1981), p. 5.4.

37. Ibid., pp. 5.3-5.4, 4.28.

7

THE ADMINISTRATION OF
THE FEDERAL AID
PROGRAM

INTRODUCTION

Responsibility for administering the federal transit aid program is lodged with the Urban Mass Transportation Administration (UMTA), a bureau of the U.S. Department of Transportation. In terms of personnel, UMTA is a relatively small bureaucracy, but it is responsible for managing the largest discretionary grant program in the civilian budget.

It is important to understand UMTA's role in the administration of transit policy because the language of the 1964 Urban Mass Transportation Act leaves room for the agency to exercise substantial discretion in awarding grants and setting transit priorities. Thus, the way in which UMTA has chosen to use its administrative discretion has had significant impact on the thrust and content of federal transit policy.

As we discuss UMTA's administration of the federal subsidy program, it is important to remember that public bureaucracies must perform and balance a multitude of roles. Bureaucracies are interpreters of legislative mandate and custodians of public funds. But they are also a medium for transmitting constituency concerns and for budget advocacy. As important, bureaucracies are a setting in which world views are cultured and refined into technocratic doctrines. As we shall see, the world view of UMTA professionals is one that emphasizes changing the structure of cities to accommodate transit instead of reorganizing transit to serve the changing demography and travel patterns of metropolitan America.

UMTA'S MISSION AND MANDATE

UMTA, like many other federal agencies, struggles with and suffers from a broad and inexplicit mandate because the legislation that created and expanded the transit assistance program provides an ill-defined guide to the purposes Congress intended to achieve by subsidizing transit. The mandate stated in the initial 1961 Act was to "assist state and local governments and their public instrumentalities in planning and providing for necessary community facilities to preserve and improve essential mass transportation services in urban and metropolitan areas."[1] It provided no further guidance that would define what service is most essential.

The purposes cited in the 1964 Act are similarly too general to inform priority setting:[2]

1. To assist in the development of improved mass transportation facilities, equipment, techniques, and methods, with the cooperation of mass transportation companies both public and private

2. To encourage the planning and establishment of areawide urban mass transportation systems needed for economical and desirable urban development, with the cooperation of mass transportation companies both public and private

3. To provide assistance to state and local governments and their instrumentalities in financing such systems to be operated by public or private mass transportation companies as determined by local needs.

Senator Williams's menu of "15 strategies which must be considered in undertaking any mass transportation program" was equally inclusive and thus too broad to serve as a guide in establishing priorities.[3] It identified projects that should find their way into the UMTA portfolio, but no criteria for choosing the most worthy. Finally, President Kennedy's message supporting federal aid for transit was equally general and permissive:

> To conserve and enhance values *in existing urban areas* is essential. But at least as important are steps to promote economic efficiency and livability *in areas of future development* [emphasis added].

> Our national welfare therefore requires the provision of good urban transportation, with the properly balanced use of private vehicles and modern mass transport to help *shape as well as serve urban growth* [emphasis added].[4]

A broad mandate creates a dilemma for an administrative agency because clearly defined goals are necessary if a line bureaucracy is to establish spending guidelines that will be accepted as legitimate by competing claimants within the program's constituency. Without clear goals, it is difficult for bureaucracies to discipline costs, determine which projects deserve funding priority, or even articulate a general programmatic thrust. Such is the dilemma UMTA has faced since its inception.[5]

THE AGENCY'S PROGRAMMATIC THRUST

A succession of administrators has struggled, more or less mightily, with the articulation of program objectives, but UMTA expenditure policy cannot realistically be described in terms of specific objectives such as increasing transit ridership or improving the industry's operating efficiency. Rather, UMTA policy consists of broad goals that are primarily procedural. The broad thrusts of UMTA's policy from 1961 through 1980 can be described as follows:[6]

Build a broad base of constituency support for transit

Showcase the efficiency and productivity that can be achieved by rapid transit using advanced rail technology

Foster the adoption of authoritative regional plans that will shape urban growth and contain urban sprawl

Defer to local authorities on the priority needs of their transit systems

Upgrade the planning and priority setting methods of local agencies

Spend resources wisely, allocating funds on the basis of demonstrated need.

We will review each of these policies in turn, but we should note at the outset that procedural goals such as these fall short of a framework for comparing the costs and benefits of proposed projects, either singly or competitively.

Building a Constituency for Transit

The UMTA program has been attentively managed "to ensure fair distribution of program assistance," with the intent of building and broadening the constituency that perceives transit as an essential public service and a political asset.[7] Program resources are prorationed among cities of different size, and UMTA officials are attentive to the program's geographic balance as well. Although rigid formulas are not used in the discretionary grant program, grant officers seem to think in terms of historically established "fair shares" and seek to avoid criticism that the program is too heavily loaded toward expenditures in the transit-dependent cities of the Northeast or large cities in general.

Grants for bus purchase and bus facilities are distributed with minimal restrictions and requirements and maximum deference to local assessment of both the level of need and the priority of different projects. Such grants are the geographic balancer of the UMTA program because buses are the backbone technology of most transit systems in the United States. Improved bus service is the most cost-effective way in which to build transit ridership—the most visible indicator of whether the program itself is effective—and the key to building support for transit in cities with less than 1 million residents.

Much larger and lumpier sums are involved in federal grants for rail transit starts or extensions. Rail starts are the most visible product of the UMTA program and, for local officials, the most coveted evidence of their own civic leadership and their city's standing among cities. The queue of applicants for rapid transit grants has been used as a basis for asserting the "need" for augmented transit appropriations and, at the same time, motivates applicant cities to support program expansion at budget time.[8] Regions that have been unable to reach the local consensus necessary to finance a rail system have been encouraged to develop downtown people movers as a first step toward rapid transit development. Such grants provide both a visible accomplishment that accrues to the credit of civic leadership and a planning activity around which to rally support for future transit investment.

Artful use of program resources to create positive imagery and political support is an essential ingredient of effective policy, and UMTA has been extraordinarily adept at the art of balancing investments so as to build both congressional constituency and local political support.

Showcasing Advanced Technology

The investment mix of the UMTA capital grant program is heavily loaded toward rail transit. Spending for rail modernization, rail extensions, and new rail rapid transit systems have accounted for more than 70 percent of UMTA capital outlays since the program's inception, in fact, 76 percent from 1965 to 1970 and 71 percent between 1971 and 1977.[9] Table 7-1 shows the modal distribution of UMTA capital grants for the period 1975 to 1978.

New rapid transit systems in Atlanta, Miami, and Baltimore are the showcase investments of the UMTA program. Indeed, the revival of interest in transit has been built around the high-technology imagery of

TABLE 7-1 The Modal Mix of UMTA Grants,
1975-1978

Purpose	1975	1976[a]	1977	1978[b]
Bus and paratransit	442	431	480	470
Rail modernization	513[c]	588[c]	384	320
Rail extensions	—[c]	—[c]	137	210
New rail systems	251	359	288	475
Total capital grants	1,208	1,378	1,289	1,475
Interstate transfer grants for transit[1]	66	553	406	645
Total capital grants	1,272	1,931	1,695	1,920

Source: Congressional Budget Office estimates cited in David E. Boyce, "Impacts of Federal Rail Transit Investment Programs on Urban Spatial Structure," from Norman J. Glickman, The Urban Impacts of Federal Policies (Baltimore: Johns Hopkins University Press, 1980).

[a] Includes transition quarter (July 1, 1976 to September 30, 1976).

[b] Estimate.

[c] Rail modernization data for 1975 and 1976 include rail extension grants.

[1] Interstate transfer grants are used primarily for new rail systems and rail extensions.

these systems and their counterparts in San Francisco and Washington, D.C. The systems noted use advanced computer controls and operate on exclusive rights-of-way, allowing them to achieve both high frequency and high speeds. One operator can oversee a 10-coach train, a significant reduction in labor requirement relative to conventional commuter railroads; electronics accommodate boarding and ticketing without conductors or ticket agents.

These technological features of modern rapid transit were seen as a recipe for increasing the reliability, speed, and capacity of transit while reducing labor costs. At the time BART and the Metros were planned, it was expected that advanced-design transit would attract sufficient patronage and achieve sufficient labor-cost economies to operate without subsidies beyond the tax contribution required for initial construction.[10] Table 7-2 charts the expectations that prevailed circa 1960.

The new rapid transit systems that UMTA has financed—or has financed at least in part—embody the technological features just described. But BART and the Metros operate at a sizable deficit. The service quality that has been realized on a day-to-day basis is not significantly different from that offered by buses allowed exclusive use of a freeway lane or priority entry at metered freeway ramps. The initial capital cost of rapid transit is significantly higher than that of high-

TABLE 7-2 The Technological Features and Performance Expected
of Rapid Transit

Technological Features	Expected Impact
Electronically assisted ticketing and boarding control	Reduction in labor costs relative to conventional commuter railroads
Exclusive rights-of-way	Higher reliability than buses operating in congested mixed traffic; speeds exceeding that of automobile or bus travel on urban freeways
Computer-controlled headways	Ability to achieve a speed-and-frequency combination competitive with the portal-to-portal travel times of the automobile
Computer-assisted one-person train crews	Reduction in labor costs relative to commuter railroads and bus service of comparable capacity
Systems effect of these technological features when combined in a modern rapid transit system	An increase in capacity, comfort, reliability, and speed deliverable at a cost lower than conventional transit and providing a level of service that allows transit to compete with the automobile on even terms

capacity bus-on-freeway transit systems; and, sadly, the economies of operation expected for rapid transit have not approached early expectations. Operating costs have been higher than expected, in large measure because savings in crew and station costs have been offset by higher than expected costs for maintenance, central control, and vehicle-warranty compliance. Patronage has been lower than predicted, in part because early patronage projections were premised on far more powerful impacts on development density and construction activity than have actually occurred.[11]

Analyses using formal economic conventions for costing show negative benefit-cost ratios for new rail systems and higher costs per passenger than for close-to-comparable bus systems.[12] At very high traffic densities, rail is cost competitive with bus service, but few American cities have traffic corridors with passenger volumes equal to the capabilities of the technology. From the standpoint of capacity, rail rapid transit can outperform express bus services, but it is an excessively costly response to the transit market in cities with settlement patterns shaped by the automobile and with the peak/off-peak traffic balance typical of the automobile era. Table 7-3, compiled by Merewitz, shows comparative cost estimates for bus and rail transit as developed by three separate research groups.

Despite the disappointing costs and performance record of new

TABLE 7-3 The Comparative Cost of Bus and Rail Transit
as of 1972

	Boyd et al.[1]	Keeler et al.[2]	Meyer et al.[3]
Rail	$3.20	$5.00	$1.41
Bus	1.50	2.75	1.13
Auto	—	4.10	1.70
Interest rate (%)	10%	12%	6%
Time value (dollars in, dollars out of vehicle)	1.2, 3	3, 9	None

Source: Leonard Merewitz, *Impacts of the Urban Mass Transportation Administration Capital Grants Program* (Washington, D.C.: National Transportation Policy Study Commission, 1979).

[1] J. Hayden Boyd, Norman Asher, and Elliot Wetzler, *Evaluation of Rail Rapid Transit and Express Bus Service in the Urban Commuter Market* (Washington, D.C.: Institute for Defense Analyses, 1973).

[2] Theodore Keeler, Leonard Merewitz, and Peter Fisher, *The Full Costs of Urban Transport*, Vols. I, II, and III (Berkeley, Calif.: University of California, Institute of Urban and Regional Development, 1975).

[3] John Meyer, John Kain, and Martin Wohl, *The Urban Transportation Problem* (Cambridge, Mass.: Harvard University Press, 1965).

rail systems, UMTA's commitment to heavy rail transit continued through the 1970s. The agency's stated rationale for investing in rapid transit has changed, however, as data on operating performance mounted. The continuing emphasis on rail investment came to be rationalized on the basis of land development impacts said to outweigh comparisons of the relative costs of bus and rail systems.

Fostering Regionalism and Shaping Urban Growth

Federal involvement in transit finance has brought with it an institution-building endeavor—an effort to foster agencies capable of authoritative planning at the *regional* or *metropolitan* level. Regionalism, as promoted by UMTA, is a means for achieving specific policy outcomes; it is not a policy-neutral institutional arrangement. UMTA's support of regionalism rests on a set of values, beliefs, and propositions that are interrelated and intertwined in the fashion of a well-developed ideology or doctrine.[13] The world view that makes up "ideological regionalism" can be described in terms of the following assertions:

Patterns of urban development on the model of San Francisco and New York are preferable to the "sprawling" development of Los Angeles or Houston.

Development at the densities typical of postwar suburbs is economically wasteful and environmentally unsound.

The culture of the automobile-based suburb and shopping center is inimical to the urbanity that characterizes the great cosmopolitan cities of the world.

Transportation not only can but *should* be used to shape the form and pattern of urban development.

Construction of rail transit systems can influence real estate development decisions in a fashion that shapes and molds the pattern of land use and the form of cities.

Authoritative planning at the regional or metropolitan scale is necessary to curb sprawl, channel areawide development, and intensify land use.

Regional planning agencies should chart the broad course of metropolitan development. They should function like architects in the design of a regional plan and like general contractors in its implementation, subcontracting with transit agencies, highway departments, cities, and counties to implement the plan.

Not all UMTA professionals embrace ideological regionalism. Many UMTA officials simply view regionalism as a logical institutional arrangement, but the prevailing organizational view is more doctrinal.[14]

UMTA's collective ideology is important because it has had significant bearing on the agency's investment priorities and its strategy for stabilizing the transit industry. The agency has emphasized growth management and rail investment as companion strategies to shape the course of urban development and thus create viable markets for mass transit. Little counterpart effort has been made to encourage transit properties to adjust their mode of operation and mix of services in a manner better suited to their residual market and their supplemental role in the scheme of urban transportation. With the exception of the Service and Methods Demonstration Program, most UMTA officials seem to have taken the structure and customs of the transit industry as a given—at least they did so until the Reagan administration. Priority went to financing the technology—heavy rail—and building the institutional machinery—regional planning—that would reshape urban settlement patterns.[15] No comparable effort was made to modernize the customs and structure of the transit industry. Such effort was simply not consistent with the normative content of the agency's dominant ideology.

Contrary to the hopes and expectations of regionalists, metropolitan planning has not been very effective or influential in accomplishing growth management.[16] In part this is because local jurisdictions have been unwilling to cede authority to regional agencies or to accede to regional plan priorities when they call for densification of development. Growth management has also faltered because most Americans, both as citizens and consumers, do not share the urbanist values of ideological regionalism. Judging by trends in population migration and interregional growth shares, most Americans find little objectionable about the life-style of the automobile-suburb-and-shopping center. Indeed, development nationwide is trending toward further suburbanization and lower densities, not toward development on the model of New York or San Francisco.[17]

Even in San Francisco and other cities with recently constructed rail transit systems, the dominant development trend is toward increasingly lower density. Rapid transit systems like BART are influencing household location decisions but are having little impact on real estate development decisions. Those impacts that have occurred are localized and are not sufficiently forceful to influence the shape and form of regional development.[18] BART's impact, for example, has not been powerful enough to reverse the continuing decline in San Francisco's and Oakland's share of total Bay Area employment.

The construction of rapid transit has had more influence on household location decisions and urban activity patterns than on the density or spatial patterns of new construction and real estate development. In San Francisco, employees are using BART to work downtown but obtain the living space, yard space, and child-rearing environment of the suburbs.[19] In fact, BART seems in a small way to be increasing the demand for the construction of housing at suburban densities. This outcome is certainly contrary to the intended goal of curbing "sprawl" and channeling urban growth in the direction of redevelopment and densification.

If expanding the housing opportunities accessible to downtown workers is a *desired* policy outcome, that objective can be achieved cost effectively by bus-on-freeway rapid transit. An evaluation of the San Bernardino busway in Los Angeles indicates that the busway was an important factor in the location choices of a significant number of households that changed their places of residence.[20] On the other hand, bus transit is apparently less attractive than rapid transit for midday shopping and recreation trips.

Despite the accumulation of evidence to the contrary, official UMTA policy hedges some but still clings to the proposition that rail transit can be a forceful instrument of growth management and intensified land use. Official UMTA policy states

> While today rail facilities are less effective in shaping land use, because automobiles have given people much greater freedom to live and work where they choose, evidence shows that when supported by appropriate zoning policies and development incentives, rail transit can still exert a strong shaping influ-

ence on the pattern of urban growth. To the extent that it can foster higher density, clustered development, rail transit can be a means to more efficient forms of urban settlement.[21]

Thus, ideological regionalism continued to shade UMTA's interpretation of the magnitude of land use impacts achievable by constructing new rapid transit systems—at least through the 1970s.

Deferring to Local Priorities

UMTA has traditionally considered grant applicants—usually transit operators—the best judge of local investment needs and priorities. UMTA does not, for example, place priorities of its own on the relative merit of a grant for buses, for a bus maintenance facility, or the hardware required for a communications center. The need for such investments and their priority is considered a proper matter for local determination. Similarly, UMTA defers to local judgment when an operator attaches higher priority to bus replacement than to service expansion, although UMTA does require grant applicants to obtain regional planning agency endorsement of the investments proposed.

Deference to the grant applicant's priorities is clearly responsive; it conforms to the commonsense principle that better informed decision makers can make better informed decisions; and it minimizes the personnel and overhead costs of federal grant review. But despite these obvious merits, there are also liabilities associated with UMTA's practice of deferring to local priorities.

Deference to local priorities means that national objectives—most notably energy conservation—can only be achieved haphazardly. Deference to local priorities also raises a significant question about whether UMTA can meaningfully set, much less achieve, national program targets such as increased ridership, increased operating efficiency, or increased mobility for the elderly and handicapped. If program targets and objectives cannot be set, competing grant applications cannot be reviewed from the viewpoint of cost-effectiveness. And that, indeed, seems to be the case: the grant review process is more responsive than it is discriminating. UMTA allocates funds on a first-come, first-served basis constrained by prorationing for the purpose of geographic balance. Grants are not awarded on the basis of true competitive merit or cost-effectiveness.[22]

When the administration of a federal grant program is designed for responsiveness rather than cost-effectiveness, it is usually appropriate to transfer the program to local control, reconstituting it as a formula rather than as a discretionary grant program. This is the logic that led Congress to reconstitute part of the capital grant program and place bus replacement on the footing of a formula grant program. It is also the logic of the New Federalism.

Upgrading the Analytic Capabilities of the Transit Industry

Upgrading the planning, market analysis, and programming skills of local agencies is the companion policy to UMTA's practice of deference to local priorities. At the inception of federal aid in 1961, not one public transit agency in the United States had a marketing department. Few had planning departments, and almost none had multiyear development plans or future-year forecasts of revenues, patronage, or potential demand. These rudimentary ingredients of service planning and market adaptation are now in place primarily because of federal involvement and, in some cases, overesistance from local operators.

Indeed, UMTA should be commended for rebuilding transit's planning capability and its role in kindling industry interest in market analysis and marketing. Significantly, though, it is the newly organized and newly staffed transit agencies that have adopted the entrepreneurial style of marketing, and not the older properties that account for the bulk of transit ridership in the United States. Few older, established properties have reconsidered the product mix they offer and its fit with the changing demography of their markets or the changing geography of urban trip making.

Allocating Resources Wisely

It is obligatory for agencies that disburse funds to include economy and cost-effectiveness in their portfolio of goals and objectives. Within UMTA, the effort to allocate resources judiciously has been undertaken seriously, not just as a ritual gesture. For reasons we will explore, that effort has produced disappointing results.

The goal of economy in government requires a disciplined approach to spending that seeks top value from each dollar spent. In the case of the capital grant program, economy would be served by a review and screening process that allows UMTA to

Negotiate with grant applicants so as to scale down outsized projects based on inflated ambitions

Rank projects on the basis of competitive merit

Reject projects that fail to meet a minimum standard of return on investment

There has been long-standing effort within UMTA to erect a programming process based on the first of these three principles. This effort has focused on creating procedures that produce disciplined plans and proposals. The agency's formal procedure involves a staged sequence of interactions between UMTA and grant applicants intended to generate grant proposals that are both well planned and economically responsible from their conception.[23] UMTA's goal has been the creation of a pool of grant applications that are virtually 100 percent worthy of assistance so they may be approved as they are received and then programmed as resources become available. The success of such an approach hinges on the self-discipline of grant applicants—and UMTA's ability to exert outside discipline on local ambitions from the start of the project planning and development process.

Outside discipline is particularly important for new rapid transit systems and significant extensions of existing rail systems. This is the case because local officials truly view rapid transit as the grand prize of the UMTA sweepstakes; 20 cents buy a dollar's worth of construction activity; and civic plaudits are to be earned throughout the planning and construction process while the tax cost of subsidized operation can be deferred for the duration. Thus there are strong incentives for localities to seek rail funding rather than pursue bus-on-freeway transit or other rubber-tired transit alternatives that are less costly than rail systems but require an early commitment to local operating subsidy.

Both local and federal officials privately agree that most rail system plans would not be proposed if localities had to pay a larger share of project costs. This is a telltale indicator that UMTA has not succeeded in its effort to build fiscal restraint into the project development process from its beginning.

Considering the constituency relationship that develops between virtually all federal agencies and the clients they serve, UMTA's difficulty restraining local ambitions should not be surprising. It is difficult in the extreme for a bureaucracy to allocate resources judiciously when the architecture of its legislation is conducive to the inflation of "needs." This is the situation UMTA faces—an 80 percent federal matching contribution that fuels the ambitions of local planning and inflates perceived needs.

If fiscal discipline is desired, the appropriate remedy is legislative—reducing the federal matching share to a lower percentage contribution. Our analysis of the behavioral dynamics of the capital grant program suggests that a 50:50 federal-local matching ratio would be more appropriate for mass transit capital grants and perhaps for federally aided public works programs in general. A 50:50 matching ratio would force localities to give more appropriate weight to the opportunity cost of the capital required for major rail investments.

Lest this analysis be misunderstood, we should emphasize that rail transit, and particularly additions to existing rail sytems, can be cost-effective when introduced in travel markets where a transit riding habit is well established, where significant off-peak traffic can be anticipated, and where the capacity of bus transit will soon be exploited to the limits of its cost advantage. We intend no categorical brief against rail transit. Rather, our concern is with the inflated cost of rail projects that are motivated by the imagery of high technology, the ambitions of local officials, or the availability of capital with little opportunity cost.

PROGRAM DESIGN AND MANAGEMENT:
A BRIEF RECAPITULATION

A program's *effectiveness*—its impact—depends, in large measure, on the resources that it can command. But a program's *cost-effectiveness* depends on how well those resources are put to use. How well resources can be put to use depends, in turn, on how well conceived, structured, and managed a program is. Program performance can be evaluated quantitatively, but there are no quantitative standards against which to measure program design and management. Nevertheless, we can ask qualitative questions with implicit normative content:

> Is the program premised on a sound diagnosis of the problems to be solved?
>
> Is it built on a realistic appraisal of the eventual cost of remedying those problems?
>
> Is it built on a realistic appraisal of the results that can be achieved with the policy instruments at its command?
>
> Is it designed to focus resources where the needs or returns are greatest?
>
> Are program managers exercising the fiscal discipline necessary to control costs?
>
> Are the program's broad thrust and budget allocation process based on clear priorities and evidence of cost-effectiveness?
>
> Has the program "learned as it evolves"? That is, has it built a knowledge base and used it to make better decisions?

Judged by these standards of conduct, qualitative as they may be, the UMTA program does not fare very well. Let us recapitulate the record:

1. The program was premised on the perception that transit's declining patronage and profitability were due to aging equipment and

unbalanced public policy—particularly spending for highways. Congressional advocates of transit subsidy misjudged the severity of transit's competitive disadvantage relative to the automobile and overstated the operating economies and ridership gains that could be achieved by reequipping the industry.

2. Congress "backed into" its commitment to transit. The eventual size of the federal obligation was not anticipated, and the cost of retrofitting the industry and halting the loss of patronage seems to have been underestimated by approximately a factor of 10.

3. The results the program could achieve—and particularly the results that could be achieved by new rail systems—were overstated. Reequipping the transit industry has not stabilized its finances: deficits continue to rise, precipitating recurrent budget crises. The land development impacts, labor-cost savings, and productivity of rapid transit have been overpromised in the extreme.

4. The resources of the program have been committed to capital-intensive investments in rail transit construction on the one hand and to a thin-spread program of operating assistance on the other. Neither the extreme concentration of capital investment nor the geographic parity of operating assistance have been cost-effective. The capital subsidy per passenger is disproportionately high for rail systems. The operating subsidy per passenger is disproportionately high for suburban and sunbelt jurisdictions.

5. The program has triggered inflated perceptions of "transit need" as localities seek grants for high-visibility rail systems. The intrinsic dynamics of an 80:20 federal local matching grant program stimulate local ambition and frustrate efforts to discipline costs. A serious effort was made to discipline costs, but that effort was overwhelmed by the constituency politics of the transit program.

6. The program has been managed to enhance legislative appeal, respond to local priorities, build the institutional machinery necessary for regional planning, and achieve transportation objectives cost effectively. But when push has come to shove, the objective of cost-effectiveness has been subordinated to UMTA's other goals.

7. UMTA has developed a knowledge base that indicates that the most cost-effective approach to mass transportation in most American communities would involve geographically specialized, market-customized services using the road network and rubber-tired technology—buses, minibuses, vans, taxis, and the shared-occupancy, privately owned automobile. This knowledge has not influenced spending priorities significantly. The program continued to commit most of its resources to high-technology, high-visibility rail systems throughout the 1970s.

NOTES

1. *Hearings on S. 345*, Subcommittee on Housing, Senate Committee on Banking and Currency, 87th Cong. (Washington, D.C.: Government Printing Office, 1961), p. 5. Senate Bill 345 was later incorporated in the Housing Act of 1961.

2. Public Law 88-364, "The Urban Mass Transportation Act of 1964," Section 2b.

3. *Hearings on S. 345*, Senate Banking Committee, pp. 29-30.

4. *Hearings on H.R. 11158*, House Committee on Banking and Currency, 87th Cong., 2nd sess. (Washington, D.C.: Government Printing Office, 1962), p. 11. A reprint of President John F. Kennedy's "Message on Transportation," delivered April 4, 1962.

5. George M. Smerk, *Urban Mass Transportation—A Dozen Years of Federal Policy* (Bloomington: Indiana University Press, 1974), pp. 250-256.

6. UMTA has never issued a comprehensive policy statement that purports to represent national urban transportation policy or federal transit policy. *De facto* policy must be inferred from regulations printed in the *Federal Register*, testimony by UMTA administrators at appropriations time, and *ex cathedra* statements made by senior officials at conferences, in memoranda, and in hearings. Our interpretation of UMTA policy is based on such sources.

7. Smerk, *Urban Mass Transportation*, pp. 253-254.

8. The initial estimates of the "need" for federal assistance and its magnitude were based on the estimated cost of constructing rapid transit systems in regions considering them in 1961, as noted in Chapter 6.

9. Leonard Merewitz, *Impacts of the Urban Mass Transportation Administration Capital Grants Program* (Washington, D.C.: National Transportation Policy Study Commission, 1979), pp. 3-7.

10. Statement of John M. Peirce, general manager, Bay Area Rapid Transit District, in *Hearings on S. 345*, Senate Banking Committee, p. 251.

11. Peat, Marwick, Mitchell & Co., *BART'S First Five Years: Transportation and Travel Impacts, Interpretive Summary* (Berkeley, Calif.: Metropolitan Transportation Commission, 1979), p. 10.

12. Merewitz, *Impacts of the Capital Grant Program*, pp. 47-49; T. E. Keeler and L. Merewitz, *The Full Costs of Urban Transport*, Vol. III (Berkeley, Calif.: Institute for Urban and Regional Development, 1976).

13. The urban transit functions of the federal government were initially lodged in the Office of Urban Transportation in the Housing and Home Finance Agency, which was later to become the Department of Housing and Urban Development. Early association with the federal government's urban renewal and comprehensive metropolitan planning initiatives had an important influence on the world view of the agency that would only later be transferred to the Department of Transportation.

14. This is a judgment based on friendships and conversations with numerous UMTA officials and professionals over a seven-year period.

15. Commitment to these priorities occurred during the Kennedy administration. See "Joint Report to the President by the Secretary of Commerce and the Housing and Home Finance Administrator," in *Hearings on H.R. 11158*, House Banking Committee, pp. 36, 46-47.

16. See, for example, David E. Boyce, *Metropolitan Planmaking* (Philadel-

phia: Regional Science Research Institute, 1970). See also David W. Jones, Jr., "The Politics of Metropolitan Transportation Planning" (Berkeley, Calif.: Institute of Transportation Studies, 1976).

17. Philip N. Fulton, "Public Transportation: Solving the Commuting Problem?" (Washington, D.C.: Transportation Research Board, 1983), pp. 9–17.

18. Robert L. Knight, "The Impact of Rail Transit on Land Use: Evidence and Change of Perspective," in Herbert S. Levinson and R. A. Weant, eds., *Urban Transportation Perspective and Prospects* (Westport, Conn.: ENO Foundation for Transportation, 1982), p. 112.

19. Metropolitan Transportation Commission, *Final Report of the BART Impact Study* (Berkeley, Calif.: MTC, 1980), p. 107.

20. John Crain and Associates, *Second Year Report, San Bernardino Freeway Express Busway Evaluation* (Los Angeles: Southern California Association of Governments, 1975), pp. 39–40.

21. Urban Mass Transportation Administration, *Policy Toward Rail Transit*, CFR 78-5813, Vol. 43, no. 45 (March 7, 1978), p. 9428.

22. John Bennett, *The UMTA Rail Modernization Program* (Washington, D.C.: U.S. Department of Transportation, 1978), pp. V.10–V.13. Bennett observes that cost-effectiveness is considered by localities weighing project priorities, but that formal competitive evaluation is not undertaken by UMTA when reviewing local grant requests.

23. The process mandated by UMTA requires the evaluation of alternatives including low-capital alternatives such as bus-on-freeway transit. The procedural requirements for alternatives analysis have been refined steadily since the publication of UMTA's *Policy Toward Rail Transit* in 1978. See also *Urban Transportation Alternatives: Evolution of Federal Policy* (Washington, D.C.: Transportation Research Board, 1977), pp. 18–35.

8

THE PERFORMANCE OF THE
FEDERAL AID PROGRAM

Critics of federal subsidy for mass transit maintain that the costs of subsidy exceed its tangible benefits. Many also argue that federal funds have been spent in a fashion that is targetless and undisciplined.[1] The advocates of subsidy counter that federal aid is justified by the importance of transit's role in congestion relief, urban renewal, urban growth management, air quality improvement, energy conservation, and the mobility that transit provides for the elderly and handicapped. They argue that subsidizing transit is much less costly than is building highways of comparable peak-hour capacity.

The promises made by the advocates of subsidy and transit's track record in redeeming them provide a framework for evaluating program performance. This was the approach used by the National Transportation Policy Study Commission (NTPSC) in the most formal and rigorous evaluation of the UMTA program that has been accomplished to date. The NTPSC evaluation was carried out by economist Leonard Merewitz and focused on the direct impacts of the capital grant program.[2] Merewitz estimated the additional ridership attributable to federal capital grants and the consequent reductions in traffic congestion, air pollution, petroleum shortfall, and traffic accidents that such investment is likely to produce in future years. Taking into account all program impacts that could be enumerated and monetized, Merewitz concluded that the UMTA program has been more costly than beneficial.

At best, Merewitz argued, the $8 billion invested to capitalize transit between 1964 and 1977 will produce only $6.8 billion in tangible benefits over the economic life of the vehicles purchased and the facilities built.[3] The rail element of the program, in particular, shows low rates of economic return. Merewitz computed a benefit-cost ratio for rail investments that falls in the range of .3 to .6, far less than the 1.0 break-even point. In contrast, the bus element of the capital grant program was computed as a break-even or better proposition with a benefit-cost ratio in the range of .75 to 1.5, after correcting for arithmetic error in Merewitz's original computation.[4]

Despite its apparent rigor, the NTPSC analysis is far from conclusive. It is inconclusive because it neglects a primary purpose and goal of the federal program.[5] As President John F. Kennedy stated the case, "Only a program that offers substantial support and continuity of Federal participation can induce our urban regions to organize appropriate administrative arrangements and meet their share of the costs of fully balanced transportation systems."[6] As this statement suggests, the merits of the federal aid program hinge on both its direct impacts *and the local initiative that it catalyzed.* Merewitz considered direct impacts only, neglecting the program's galvanizing effect on localities.

Unfortunately, we cannot know with any confidence how transit would have performed and localities responded in the absence of federal intervention. We can guess that the decline of ridership would have continued, that local governments would have been less universally motivated to assume ownership of failing private properties, that fewer localities would have provided subsidies for day-to-day operations of transit service, and that total subsidy would have summed to a lesser amount. But we cannot know with any certainty the degree to which this would have been the case. Analyses of the sort performed by Merewitz rely on a baseline constructed with artificial certainty—and thus provide a less than reliable measure of actual program impacts and true program performance.

For this reason, we will concentrate on whittling down the uncertainty associated with knowing how transit would have fared in the absence of federal intervention. We can begin that analysis by examining the trend of ridership in the relatively sluggish start-up phase of the UMTA program—1960 to 1970—and comparing it with the ridership trend of the 1970s, the period of dramatically increasing subsidy. Table 8-1 compares the trend of work-trip ridership in these two periods for 20 major transit markets. As can be seen, universal decline was the norm for the decade of the 1960s, whereas a mixed performance pattern is evident in the decade of the 1970s.

During both decades—that of the 1960s and that of the 1970s— the resident population of those cities that are today's major transit markets was in steady decline. Table 8-2 shows that transit ridership for

TABLE 8-1   Trend of Work-Trip Ridership
in Major Transit Markets,
1960-1970 and 1970-1980

Metropolitan Area	Percentage Change	
	1960–1970	1970–1980
Atlanta	−32.1%	+4.3%
Baltimore	−20.2	−1.0
Boston	−24.6	+.3
Buffalo	−37.5	−4.7
Chicago	−39.0	+6.0
Cincinnati	−46.2	+.2
Cleveland	−37.8	4.4
Denver	−41.5	+7.7
Detroit	−36.5	−20.7
Kansas City	−52.7	−20.7
Los Angeles	−33.1	+14.3
Miami	−13.3	+.3
Milwaukee	−39.5	−5.4
Minneapolis	−22.5	+4.6
New Orleans	−27.5	−5.9
New York	−24.7	−39.4
Philadelphia	−37.6	−11.7
St. Louis	−50.1	−1.4
San Francisco	−14.6	+18.0
Seattle	−24.6	+9.1
Washington, D.C.	−13.9	+12.9

Source: Bureau of the Census, *Statistical Abstract of the United States, 1981* (Washington, D.C.: Government Printing Office, 1981).

the journey to work declined faster than resident urban population in the 1960s, whereas the reverse was true in the 1970s. In the 1970s, transit was more successful in holding and attracting ridership than were its host cities in retaining resident population. Table 8-2 is important in two respects. On the one hand, it indicates that transit's performance is not terribly important to the stability of urban neighborhoods; indeed, there is no correlation between transit performance and central-city population stability. On the other hand, Table 8-2 also suggests that subsidy afforded many properties the wherewithal to buck the forceful downtrend of central-city population, allowing them to increase ridership in the face of a declining market base.

If we normalize the transit ridership statistics of Table 8-2 in a fashion that accounts for population decline, we see that transit ridership increased relative to its central-city market base in every major market except one—metropolitan New York. The adjusted net is shown

TABLE 8-2 Trend of Work-Trip Ridership and Central-City Population, 1960–1970 and 1970–1980

Metropolitan Area	1960–1970		1970–1980	
	Percentage Ridership Change	Percentage Change in Core City Population	Percentage Ridership Change	Percentage Change in Core City Population
Atlanta	−32.1%	+2.1%	+4.3%	−14.1%
Baltimore	−20.2	−3.5	−1.0	−13.1
Boston	−24.6	−8.0	+.3	−12.2
Buffalo	−37.5	−13.1	−4.7	−22.7
Chicago	−39.0	−5.2	+6.0	−10.8
Cincinnati	−46.2	−9.9	+.2	−10.8
Cleveland	−37.8	−14.3	−4.4	−23.6
Denver	−41.5	+4.3	+7.7	−4.3
Detroit	−36.5	−9.5	−20.7	−16.7
Kansas City	−52.7	+6.5	+.2	−11.7
Los Angeles	−33.1	+13.6	+14.3	+5.5
Miami	−13.3	−14.7	+.3	+3.6
Milwaukee	−39.7	−3.2	−5.4	−11.3
Minneapolis	−22.5	−10.1	+4.6	−14.6
New Orleans	−27.5	−5.6	−5.9	−6.1
New York	−24.7	+1.5	−39.4	−10.4
Philadelphia	−37.6	−2.7	−11.7	−13.4
St. Louis	−50.1	−17.1	−1.4	−27.2
San Francisco	−14.6	−3.2	+18.0	−5.1
Seattle	−24.6	−4.7	+9.1	−5.1
Washington, D.C.	−13.9	−.9	+12.9	−15.6

Source: Bureau of the Census, *Statistical Abstract and Census of Population, Subject Reports: Journey to Work, 1970 and 1980* (Washington, D.C.: Government Printing Office, 1973 and 1983).

in Table 8-3; it provides persuasive evidence that subsidy has produced more significant returns than would be calculated without taking demographic change into account. Our conclusion is that subsidy was a more powerful instrument in retaining and attracting ridership than Merewitz and other critics of the federal program have credited. But another implication of Table 8-3 is that transit subsidy had only a palliative effect on the stability of central-city neighborhoods. In fact, it could be reasonably argued that federal aid induced cities to spend too much on transit at the expense of other programs that could have made a more effective contribution to the stability of urban neighborhoods.

From this analysis we conclude that *the critics of transit subsidy have understated the ridership and transportation impacts of the federal program, whereas the proponents of subsidy have overstated its merits as a strategy of urban revitalization.* The understatement of transportation benefits is the result of computing impacts and thus benefits against an overly sanguine baseline. Subsidy not only increased ridership, but it increased it in the face of a shrinking central-city market base. In the absence of federal intervention and the incentive it provided for local initiative on the transit front, continuing ridership loss

TABLE 8-3 Trend of Transit Ridership Normalized
for Population Change, 1970–1980

Metropolitan Area	Percentage Change in Ridership Less Percentage Change in Central-City Population
Atlanta	+18.4%
Baltimore	+12.1
Boston	+12.5
Buffalo	+8.0
Chicago	+16.8
Cincinnati	+11.0
Cleveland	+19.2
Denver	+11.3
Detroit	+4.0
Kansas City	+11.9
Los Angeles	+8.8
Miami	+3.3
Milwaukee	+5.9
Minneapolis	+19.2
New Orleans	+.2
New York	−29.0
Philadelphia	+1.7
St. Louis	+25.8
San Francisco	+23.1
Seattle	+14.2
Washington, D.C.	+5.9

and declining transportation contribution would almost certainly have resulted. Thus, subsidy produced more significant results than its critics credit.

Reconsidering the baseline used for impact assessment leads to the conclusion that the benefits produced by the UMTA program have been roughly commensurate with the cost of federal aid. The program emerges as a cost-effective one if it is credited with employing central-city workers who would otherwise have been unemployed or under-employed. Using shadow prices for transit labor costs leads to the conclusion that the program has produced benefits in excess of its cost.

While we must reject Merewitz's conclusion that subsidy has cost more than it is worth, we cannot quarrel with his subsidiary conclusion that the cost-effectiveness of the program has been diminished by its emphasis on rapid transit systems in the mold of the Atlanta, Baltimore, and Miami Metros.

Having dealt with program's overall yield, it is appropriate to examine its priorities in greater detail. Tables 8-2 and 8-3 provide a starting point for this analysis: Table 8-2 showed the market performance of properties in different cities, and Table 8-3 showed, in effect, how well transit properties have been able to cope with change in their market base. These tables provide a kind of crude measure of the market performance and the management performance of transit properties in 20 major regions. Absolute change in ridership offers a proxy for market performance, whereas ridership change adjusted for population change offers a proxy for management performance, that is, management's ability to cope with change.

Table 8-4 shows a ranking of federal transit expenditures by city and a ranking of transit's market and mangement performance in the same cities.[7] It allows us to ask whether federal investment has rewarded properties in those cities where transit and its management are performing best. As is evident from Table 8-4, there is little correspondence between federal expenditure level and transit performance.

Table 8-5 shows those metropolitan areas that have received federal funding greater than their performance ranking would merit and those that have received less. It shows midsized regions receiving less than a performance-based share of federal allocations and apportionments, whereas New York, Philadelphia, Detroit, Boston, and Chicago have received shares larger than those that would be merited by recent performance. Our intent is not to criticize transit management in the latter cities; rather, we wish to learn something about federal investment priorities—whether the federal dollar is being spent where transit and its management are performing best. Table 8-5 is instructive in this regard.

Regions that have received outsized federal assistance relative to

TABLE 8-4 Rank Ordering of Metropolitan Areas
by Share of Federal Outlays, Ridership Trend and Adjusted Ridership Trend,
1970–1980

Metropolitan Area	Ranking by[1] Share of Federal Outlays	Market Performance: Ranking by 1970–1980 Ridership Change	Management Performance: 1970–1980 Adjusted Ridership Change
New York	1	21	21
Washington, D.C.	2	3	1
Boston	3	10	10
Chicago	4	6	8
Philadelphia	5	19	19
Atlanta	6	8	6
San Francisco	7	1	3
Baltimore	8	13	11
Los Angeles	9	2	15
Miami	10	9	18
Detroit	11	20	17
Cleveland	12	15	14
Buffalo	13	16	7
Seattle	14	4	9
Denver	15	5	13
Minneapolis	16	7	5
St. Louis	17	14	2
New Orleans	18	18	20
Cincinnati	19	12	14
Milwaukee	20	17	16
Kansas City	21	11	12

[1] Data on federal outlays for public transportation is from U.S. House of Representatives, Committee on Public Works and Transportation, *Oversight of the Federal Public Transportation Assistance Program* (Washington, D.C.: Government Printing Office, 1982).

the performance of their transit systems are those with the nation's largest transit properties. Collectively, they account for 44 percent of nationwide transit patronage. Table 8-6 shows how these transit operations rank in terms of fleet size nationwide. Each of these properties is by reputation either "unmanageable" or "remarkably well managed considering their impossible situation." They are simultaneously the most important and among the most troubled properties in the nation. Paradoxically, size accounts for both their importance—and many of their problems.

Taken together, Tables 8-5 and 8-6 suggest that an implicit, but operative, rule governing federal expenditure has been the allocation of more funds to those transit systems that are most troubled rather than to those where the opportunity to increase ridership is most promising.

TABLE 8-5 Metropolitan Areas Receiving Substantially More
or Less Federal Outlays than Would Be Expected
on the Basis of Performance Ranking,
1970–1980

Regions Receiving More Federal Assistance than Warranted by Both Market and Management Performance	Regions Receiving Less Federal Assistance than Warranted by Both Market and Management Performance
New York	Minneapolis
Philadelphia	St. Louis
Detroit	Kansas City
Boston	Seattle
Chicago	Cincinnati
	San Francisco
	Milwaukee

Funding has gone to the "most needy" rather than to the "most promising" systems. Implicit in this pattern of allocation is the premise that a monetary transfusion will stabilize troubled systems and that such systems are most deserving of federal assistance. This is a perverse allocation rule because it serves to shelter and protect the largest systems from the painful reorganization necessary to increase their productivity and restore their manageability.

Where does this analysis leave us? Has the federal aid program performed well or poorly? Let us summarize our conclusions:

1. The costs and benefits of transit subsidy are roughly commensurate.
2. The critics of federal subsidy have underestimated its impact on transit ridership whereas the advocates of subsidy have overstated its value as an urban revitalization strategy.

TABLE 8-6 Size of Operations Receiving More Federal Funds
than Performance Would Justify, 1980

Market	Major Property	Fleet Size	Nationwide Fleet-Size Ranking
New York	CTA	4,558	1
Philadelphia	SEPTA	2,540	3
Detroit	SEMTA	1,599	8
Boston	MBTA	1,774	6
Chicago	CTA	3,520	2

Source: Urban Mass Transportation Administration, *National Urban Mass Transportation Statistics* (Washington, D.C.: Government Printing Office, 1982).

3. The federal aid program has given expenditure priority to those transit systems that are most troubled rather than to those that are most effectively managed. This pattern of expenditures has sheltered transit from wrenching change, but it has also postponed necessary changes in the industry's customs and structure.

Our assessment of the performance of the federal transit aid program sums to the conclusion that it is a flawed, but not failed, initiative. Revisions in the program's thrust and content are needed, but retreat from federal involvement or the withdrawal of federal operating subsidies would be counterproductive.

NOTES

1. See, for example, George W. Hilton, *Federal Transit Subsidies* (Washington, D.C.: American Enterprise Institute, 1974); and Jose A. Gomez-Ibanez, "Assessing the Arguments for Urban Transit Operating Subsidies," in Herbert S. Levinson and Robert A. Weant, eds., *Urban Transportation: Perspectives and Prospects* (Westport, Conn.: ENO Foundation for Transportation, 1982).

2. Leonard Merewitz, *The Impacts of Urban Mass Transportation Administration Capital Grant Programs* (Washington, D.C.: National Transportation Policy Study Commission, 1979).

3. Ibid., p. 47.

4. Ibid., pp. 47–49.

5. See Senator Harrison Williams's commentary on the objectives of federal aid in Subcommittee on Housing, Senate Banking and Currency Committee, *Hearings on S. 345* (Washington, D.C.: Government Printing Office, 1961), p. 36.

6. House Committee on Banking and Currency, *Hearings on H.R. 11158* (Washington, D.C.: Government Printing Office, 1962), p. 12.

7. The federal expenditure data on which Table 8-4 is based include both capital and operating subsidies; the table thus includes both discretionary and statutory expenditures of the Urban Mass Transportation Assistance Program. The data on which the table is based was reported in *Oversight of the Federal Public Transportation Assistance Program*, House Committee on Public Works and Transportation (Washington, D.C.: Government Printing Office, 1982), p. 34. It was prepared for the committee by the Congressional Budget Office.

9

WHAT HAVE WE LEARNED?

What have we learned from our investigation of transit's history and our assessment of federal transit policy? First, transit's financial distress is a long-term and persistent phenomenon. Second, there is a mismatch between the architecture of transit operations and the composition of transit's residual market. Third, there is a mismatch between the growth rates of transit operating costs and the growth potential of its revenue base. And, finally, subsidy has not restored transit to a stable competitive footing.

A complex constellation of factors accounts for transit's persistent and continuing financial distress:

1. The inability to price service at cost without significant loss of ridership
2. The loss of seasonal, off-peak and weekend ridership, ridership that historically generated the revenue necessary to counterbalance the cost of providing peak-hour service
3. The obligation to expand peak-hour service despite the inability to use labor or equipment productively during the midday off peak
4. The inability to deflect demands for the extension of service to thin markets incompatible with the industry's cost structure
5. The loss of short-distance ridership attributable to unbalanced fare policies and the attenuation of headways

6. The decline of central-city population and the consequent erosion of the industry's primary market base

7. The preservation of established work rules, fare structures, and operating conventions despite dramatic change in the balance and composition of the industry's traffic base

8. The steady increase of base wages despite the industry's declining productivity.

As this itemization suggests, there are two primary dimensions to the problem of transit's financial distress. One can be characterized as *structural obsolescence*. The industry's cost structure, its operating customs, and its labor agreements date to the period in which transit was the dominant mode of urban transportation; its cost structure and its traffic base no longer match.

The second primary dimension of transit's financial distress is the *persistent differential between the growth rates of costs and revenues*. The real wages of transit workers increased at an average annual rate of 1.8 during the 1960s and 1970s while productivity was declining at an average annual rate of 1 percent. Stabilizing the industry would require wage restraint and sustained productivity improvement, but achieving sustained productivity improvement will be extraordinarily difficult due to institutional constraints. The two most important constraints are (1) the size and consequent unmanageability of the properties that serve the industry's most promising markets and (2) the ability of organized interests to frustrate change.

The scale of the industry's dominant properties is a roadblock to change and renewal, because managing the day-to-day operations of these large properties is an overwhelming task. Little intellectual or managerial energy is left over for thinking about, much less implementing, fundamental change in service mix, pricing strategy, labor agreements, or route structure. The size of the largest, and most troubled, operations is simply incompatible with the scrutiny of local submarkets, the constant reevaluation of routes and schedules, and the market-responsive adjustment of work rules, service levels, prices, and product mix. Little wonder, then, that transit has been slow to adapt to social, economic, and demographic change. Management's coping ability is exhausted by the overwhelming demands of day-to-day operation.

Management is also constrained by the political sensitivity of any change in service, fares, work rules, or craft agreements. The continuing decline of central-city services is, ironically enough, at least partially attributable to the political influence of those with the greatest stake in the preservation of such service: transit's riders, its workers, and the downtown establishments of the cities that it serves. The political influence of these groups protects three incompatible, but tradition-vested, entitlements: low fares, wage increases in excess of cost-of-living adjustment, and the expansion of peak-hour service. The felt need to honor these three incompatible entitlements embroils transit management in a recursive exercise in shoring, patching, and backpedaling.

The drama of shoring and patching has been played out in city after city in the era of public ownership; it can be characterized as follows. With stable fares and rising labor costs, passenger revenues are unable to keep pace with the growth of the property's wage bill. A fare increase or service reduction must be considered. The discussion of increased fares mobilizes public reaction, generating civic and political pressure for a "better alternative." One such alternative is increased subsidy. A proposal to increase subsidy is received skeptically, but it gradually emerges as the preferred option through artful packaging. The packaging that proves acceptable includes a relatively small increase in subsidy, a mild fare increase, improvements in peak-hour commuter service, and reductions in poorly patronized off-peak service. The combination of service improvements and service reductions is presented as a rationalization program, but its net result is an increase in the property's operating and capital cost obligations because of the high cost of additional peak-hour service. Passenger revenues increase proportionately less than do newly occasioned costs, and thus the financial cushion afforded by additional subsidy and higher fares is exhausted in short order. The deftly packaged plan that had been presented as a long-term solution to the property's financial woes proves durable for only a short time—perhaps two or three years. Management recognizes that a precipitous new request for additional subsidy would be rebuffed; further economy measures must be taken first. Thus, nighttime and weekend services are reduced yet again, producing modest savings. More important than their magnitude, these economies mobilize no influential constituencies and, more important still, symbolize and communicate management's resolve to control and reduce costs. Management has shored and patched; the property has demonstrated its resolve to cut and prune; it is positioned for the cycle to begin anew.

Such is the role of organized constituencies in constraining management's options and limiting change to ritual initiatives. The outcome is perverse: the property now operates less service at higher unit cost and requires proportionately greater subsidy. Indeed, subsidy will eventually account for a greater proportion of the property's operating revenues than passenger fares. This only compounds management's dilemma. Should further subsidy not be forthcoming in the future, a precipitous fare increase would be necessary to pay the property's wage bill because of the now reduced contribution of fares to the property's operating budget. Thus, the property becomes increasingly more dependent on political goodwill for the resolution of each succeeding financial emergency. This dependence inevitably colors day-to-day decision making and further delimits the boundaries of management discretion and organizational change. Once, again, we see why transit has been slow to adapt to social, economic, and demographic change and why it has been unable to achieve sustained productivity improvement. Not only is the scale of the problem overwhelming, but management's options are severely constrained by the political influence of organized urban constituencies.

We have learned, then, that transit's way of doing business is an artifact of the industry's developmental history and the politics of vested entitlement. We have also learned that stabilizing the industry will require change far more fundamental than that contemplated by Congress or local officialdom. And, finally, we have learned a pragmatic lesson: that fundamental change is unlikely unless it can be orchestrated in a fashion that revises vested entitlements without breaching them.

With this summary, we are close to understanding the requisites of transit stabilization. Stabilizing transit will require sustained productivity improvement. Achieving sustained productivity gains will, in turn, require change in the industry's structure and operating policies, but mobilizing support for change will require the preservation of entitlements.

10

THE CHALLENGE OF
STABILIZATION

INTRODUCTION

The transit policies pursued in the 1960s and 1970s were designed to preserve transit service and provide the financial support necessary for service expansion. These policies were only partially successful. Subsidy temporarily reversed the erosion of transit ridership, but the root causes of the industry's financial distress were left unaddressed. Tax support provided a financial reprieve, but it did not restore transit to a stable competitive footing. Indeed, the steadily increasing subsidy necessary to sustain transit's ridership recovery provides telling evidence that the policies of the 1960s and 1970s responded to the symptoms rather than to the causes of transit's continuing financial distress.

Stabilizing mass transit will require an artful mix of change and preservation. Change in transit's basic way of doing business is needed to increase productivity and overcome structural obsolescence—the mismatch between markets and services. Preservation is a pragmatic necessity because reorganization cannot be accomplished without building the consensus that change is acceptable and desirable.

SIX GOALS FOR TRANSIT

What must be changed, and what preserved? Our prescription follows from the accumulative diagnostic content of previous chapters. That diagnosis leads to the conclusion that restoring mass transit to a stable footing will require

1. Reestablishing manageability
2. Matching services to markets more effectively and efficiently
3. Restraining cost escalation
4. Achieving sustained productivity improvement
5. Preserving reasonable continuity of service and fares
6. Preserving the economic welfare of the transit worker.

The dilemma is that today's transit systems cannot achieve these six goals simultaneously. This is their crucial failing. As we have seen, public subsidy has allowed transit properties to preserve service, maintain low fares, and pay increasing wages but at steadily increasing expense to the general taxpayer. Management's authority to manage has been weakened as has its ability to control the deployment of service. In the era prior to public subsidy, rising costs, declining productivity, and declining revenues forced properties to curtail service and reduce their work forces. Many of today's systems are hybrid cases that evidence both dynamics simultaneously. They require more and more subsidy to provide less and less service. The unavoidable lesson of history is that stabilization cannot be accomplished without fundamental change in the way in which transit is organized and operated. What follows is our best judgment of what must be accomplished—our agenda for change and preservation.

Making Transit Manageable

Many of the most important transit operations in the nation are agglomerates—massive operations assembled by the merger and amalgamation of once-independent properties. These agglomerates serve vast metropolitan territories, and many operate fleets that exceed 1,000 vehicles. Their size and territorial reach virtually assure that such operations cannot be responsive to localized market opportunities. Their scale also serves to deter innovation because management's limited time and energy are necessarily absorbed by the overwhelming demands of day-to-day operation. The size of the nation's largest properties is simply dysfunctional. This becomes evident when we compare the largest systems with those that are the industry's leading innovators. The innovative properties in the transit industry—Portland's Tri-Met, Seattle's Metro, San Francisco's Golden Gate, San Diego's City Transit Corp., and the Transit Commission of Minneapolis–St. Paul—are all systems of manageable size and scale. The markets they serve are inherently no more promising than the markets served by the larger systems of the older industrial states. Nonetheless, their recent performance is notably superior. What distinguishes these operations is the quality of their management—and their inherent manageability. Each is small enough that system and procedure have not crowded out enterprising management or cooperative labor-management relations. All have unusually high morale and are known for driver courtesy and superior reliability. Each monitors operating performance attentively, and service adjustments are made frequently. Management evidences a tactile feel for the idiosyncrasies of local submarkets, and staff is encouraged to experiment with innovations in pricing, marketing, and operations. Finally, planning is approached from a marketing rather than an engineering perspective. The lesson to be learned from the midsized innovators is that the scale of the larger operations can be dysfunctional. The size of the largest properties defeats manageability, deters service adjustment, and encourages entrenchment rather than experimentation.

Restoring manageability—and, with it, adaptivity and entrepreneurship—to transit systems in the largest urban markets will require reorganization and decentralization. Delegation of more authority for planning, budgeting, and marketing to geographically decentralized units within the parent organization is needed to recoup the manageability that existed prior to agglomeration. In this sense, the San Francisco Bay Area with its seven independent operating properties is a more apt organizational model for regional transit service than are the metropolitan transit authorities of New York, Chicago, Boston, or Washington, D.C. Even in the Bay Area, however, the bus systems serving San Francisco and Oakland are arguably too large and complex to be managed effectively and responsively. Devolving more authority for planning, budgeting, and marketing to localized operations or localized operating subunits is, in short, a prerequisite of manageability and thus of stabilization.

Matching Services to Markets

We have emphasized that the way the transit industry does business is a product of its developmental history. The fare structure, service standards, work rules, craft structure, and labor contracts with which transit operates today have been inherited from the era of the electric street railway and the horsecar before it. In the street railway era, transit was the dominant mode of urban transportation and was used for the full range of travel purposes—travel for recreation and shopping as well as the journey to work. During transit's formative years, the demand for peak-hour service was counterbalanced by midday and weekend traffic. Indeed, Sunday was the day of heaviest transit patronage through 1900 and Saturday through the 1920s. Today, of course, most transit usage occurs during the morning and evening rush hours for the purpose of getting to work.

While the composition of transit's ridership has changed dramatically, there has not been a corresponding change in the industry's structure. It continues to operate with a fare structure, work rules, service philosophy, and craft structure appropriate to the period in which its traffic was temporally balanced and spatially concentrated.

The typical urban transit property offers a common form of service to all passengers at an essentially uniform fare, undifferentiated by time of day or the distance traveled. Service is operated on fixed routes and against fixed schedules. Headways are adjusted by time of day, but fares, fleet mix, route structure, and dispatching procedures are essentially uniform throughout the day. The result is a pattern of pricing and service delivery poorly matched to both off-peak and short-distance trip making.

The "peaking" of transit's residual traffic is equally problematic. The service and capacity requirements of the peak essentially fix transit's equipment and labor bill at an excessively costly level because neither labor nor equipment can be used productively during the mid-day hours. In turn, any expansion of peak-hour service entails an extraordinarily high unit cost.

The challenge posed by peaking and the loss of off-peak and short-distance patronage is to revise the industry's fare structure, its off-peak marketing strategy, and those contract provisions that preclude the use of permanent part-time operators. The appropriate fare structure revision would entail more general use of zone fares and peak-hour surcharges. The strategy necessary to rebuild off-peak ridership involves service differentiation—the adoption of different routing, dispatching, and scheduling procedures for the off-peak market. Table 10-1 compares conventional service with differentiated or market-specialized services.

The appropriate strategy of service differentiation will vary from market to market—and among submarkets. Nevertheless, a generalization can be risked: matching service to markets through product and price differentiation and the use of part time labor is the single most promising strategy for building and retaining patronage without incurring excessive unit costs. Making productive uses of otherwise idle labor and equipment is the key to building ridership without additional subsidy. The role of price differentiation in retaining patronage is equally important. There are notable differences in the price sensitivity of peak and off-peak and short- and long-distance riders. Across-the-board fare increases discourage transit use by disproportionate numbers of short-distance and off-peak patrons. Indeed, flat fares have contributed significantly to the erosion of short-distance ridership. In short, both price and service differentiation are requisites of transit stabilization.

TABLE 10-1 Conventional versus Differentiated Service

A. Conventional Transit Service

1. A common form of service is offered to all passengers at an essentially uniform fare.

2. The service is operated on fixed routes.

3. Headways are adjusted by time of day, but fares, fleet mix, route structure, and dispatching procedures are essentially uniform throughout the day.

4. The responsibilities of operating personnel are limited to coach operation, with limited assistance to passengers: supplying information and vouchers good for transfer, and aiding the disabled.

B. Differentiated Service

1. Service is differentiated by time of day or day of the week.

   a. Routes as well as headways vary:

      (1) Some routes are served during the peak but not during the midday.

      (2) Some routes are served during the midday, but not during the rush hour.

      (3) Some routes have no evening service.

      (4) Some routes are served on weekends only.

      (5) Some routes are served seasonally but not year-round.

2. Service is offered on the basis of advanced reservation, subscription, or charter.

   a. Charter services are offered for organized group travel.

   b. Employers are able to contract for special commute services on a contract or cost-sharing basis.

   c. Patrons are able to reserve seats by joining a club bus on a subscription basis.

3. Services offer the patrons special assistance as a standard feature of the service provided.

   a. Drivers will leave their seats to assist elderly or handicapped persons in boarding the vehicle.

   b. Drivers will leave the vehicle to provide assistance in handling luggage or packages.

   c. Bicyclists are allowed to transport their cycle on- or off-board transit vehicles.

   d. Drivers are trained to provide sightseeing commentary for tour groups.

4. Price differentiation exists.

   a. Special classes of riders—schoolchildren, the elderly, the handicapped—are afforded service at a reduced fare.

TABLE 10-1 (continued)

b. Fare-free shuttle services are operated within major activity centers.

c. Riders are able to travel during the midday at a reduced fare.

d. Premium fares are charged for express or limited-stop service.

e. Riders must pay a rush-hour surcharge for travel during the peak period.

f. Fares reflect the distance traveled.

5. Fleet is differentiated by traffic density and travel purpose.

  a. Service is provided by a mixed fleet that may include

   (1) Articulated buses

   (2) Mini- or microbuses

   (3) Tour or charter buses

   (4) Vehicles with cargo compartments

   (5) Vans

   (6) Limousines

  b. The property's fleet mix is shaped by the service requirements of off-peak travel as well as the capacity requirements of the peak.

6. Community-level service is operated without fixed route or fixed schedule.

  a. Patrons are able to obtain taxilike service routed and scheduled in response to telephone request.

  b. Riders may obtain taxilike service scheduled on a next-day, advance-reservation basis.

  c. Vehicles boarded on a main street will deliver passengers to their doorstep on an adjoining sidestreet.

7. Service is differentiated by producer cost.

  a. Some services are procured in contract arrangements with private operators or other service vendors.

  b. Agreements are reached to share tax subsidies with social service agencies that can provide paratransit services for groups with special needs.

  c. Arrangements are made to vacate routes or territories when service can be offered more economically by another operator.

  d. When the density of demand is insufficient to support service operated by a paid driver, the property is prepared to assist the formation of carpools, van pools and other ride-sharing arrangements.

Restraining Cost Escalation

As we have seen, there is a mismatch between the growth rates of transit costs and revenues. Because labor costs bulk so large in the scheme of transit expenses, restraining cost escalation will require restraint in the growth of unit labor costs. The steady increase of unit labor costs reflects two factors: transit's declining productivity and labor's success in bargaining for wage increases that exceed cost-of-living adjustment. From 1960 to 1980, for instance, unit labor costs as measured by bus driver compensation per seat mile increased 40 percent in real dollar terms. But, during the same period, compensation *per employee* increased only a modest 9 percent.

Restraining the growth of unit labor costs could be accomplished through wage restraint or sustained productivity improvement, since *unit* labor costs measure both actual payroll costs *and* system productivity. Considering the relatively modest *per employee* gains realized by transit workers in the past two decades, it is more appropriate to focus on productivity improvement than on wage restraint. But achieving sustained productivity improvement is no small problem. Indeed, the magnitude of the challenge is simply overwhelming: an annual productivity improvement of some 2.8 percent would have been necessary to offset the growth of unit labor costs that occurred in the 1960s and 1970s—a rate of productivity improvement substantially greater than the average in the manufacturing sector. Productivity gains of such magnitude are virtually unimaginable, particularly considering that the industry's productivity *declined* an average of 1 percent each year during the last two decades.

At the heart of both the productivity and labor cost problems is a fundamental structural dilemma. The transit industry is organized in a fashion that affords its workers few opportunities to better their standard of living by advancing to positions of increasing productivity or responsibility. The industry's wage structure also provides little incentive for labor to ally itself with new procedures or technologies that would increase productivity. This is because the industry is virtually devoid of career ladders or promotion opportunities that reward better performance or greater responsibility with higher pay. Instead, the typical transit worker reaches the top end of the industry's pay scale after a year or less on the job. Further increases in take-home pay can be achieved in only three ways. There is room for a small fraction of the work force to advance to positions as street supervisors, and long-standing employees can use their seniority to pick assignments that maximize the likelihood of overtime pay, but the majority of the work force has only one way to "do a little better"—supporting efforts to bargain for increases in the base wage rate. In short, increases in the base wage rate and in fringe benefits bear essentially the full burden of bettering the transit worker's standard of living.

Since the top of the pay scale is reached so early in a transit worker's career, the pressure to increase the base wage is intense. As we have said, this is because wage gains through promotion to positions of increasing responsibility are unavailable as an alternative to steady upward adjustment of the base wage. In turn, the reasons that promotion opportunities are unavailable is (1) the essential uniformity of service and (2) craft agreements that preclude cross-training and hyphenated work assignments such as operator-mechanic, operator-cashier, or operator-accountant. Transit workers must bargain for higher base wages because of a poverty of economic betterment alternatives.

The transit worker's poverty of alternatives is a vestige of turn-of-the-century labor relations and nineteenth-century technology. The work force of that period was a bifurcated one, with skilled labor performing electrification and maintenance tasks and low-skilled, primarily immigrant labor serving as coach operators. The result was the erection of impermeable craft barriers that typically precluded promotion from operating to maintenance roles or from operations to administration. The formal barriers of craft specialization were reinforced by coincident stratification and segregation on ethnic lines. These barriers persist today, as does the caste system of ethnic stratification, especially in the older urban properties.

Craft specialization and ethnic stratification have two perverse effects: (1) coach operators who are idled during the midday cannot be used productively in other work roles, and (2) career paths that lead from coach operation into maintenance or administration are generally unavailable as advancement opportunities. If such advancement opportunities were available, coach operators could improve their standard of living by training into more demanding work roles and receiving higher pay for such assignments. A laddered promotion system based on mid-career retraining has merit because the increasingly well-educated transit worker of the modern era is a promising candidate for more demanding work roles. He or she would be better off for the increase in skills and income—and transit properties would be better off for the increase in productivity. Laddered promotion might also afford the opportunity to restrain the steady growth of base wages without jeopardizing the coach operator's ability to "do a little better each year."

Career ladder promotion systems based on an intentional policy of human resource development, cross-training, and a corresponding system of merit pay increases is the way the information industries exercise wage restraint while increasing both productivity and the worker's standard of living. The differences between laddered advancement and

the compressed career opportunities available in the transit industry are
highlighted in Table 10-2, which emphasizes the linkage among productivity, innovation, and laddered promotion systems. We hypothesize
that a laddered promotion system would increase productivity and provide a framework for allying transit labor with innovations that simultaneously increase productivity and create new rungs at the top of the
promotion ladder, but the hypothesis is an untested one. This is because personnel development, cross-training, and merit pay increases are

**TABLE 10-2 Compressed versus Laddered Advancement Opportunities
Two Models**

Compressed Advancement Opportunities:
The Transit Industry Norm

A minimal spread exists between the hourly wages of entry-level and senior
workers.

There are few opportunities to increase take-home pay by promotion or training into positions of increasing responsibility.

Craft barriers prevent cross-training of operating, maintenance, and administrative personnel.

Seniority is used to pick assignments that minimize stress or maximize the
opportunity to obtain overtime pay.

Early burnout for operating personnel, with attendant pressures for higher
earning cycle wages and early retirement policies, is common.

Obtaining base wage increases in excess of cost-of-living adjustment is the only
opportunity for most workers to improve their standard of living.

Laddered Promotion, Personnel Development, and Cross-Training:
An Alternative

Widen the spread between the hourly wages of entry-level and senior workers.

Create career paths and promotion ladders to permit workers to advance or
train into positions of increasing responsibility.

Provide midcareer training and cross-training to create promotion paths within
the organization while reducing idle time on the job.

Reward increasing responsibility with merit raises.

Increase take-home pay through sustained productivity improvement.

Provide innovations that increase productivity and create new rungs on the
promotion ladder, potentially at both entry and advanced levels.

Provide financial incentive for labor to participate in productivity improvements that create new rungs on the promotion ladder.

Make sure that workers can better their standard of living without base wage
increases that exceed cost-of-living adjustment.

---

essentially foreign to the transit industry. Even the most innovative properties operate with compressed wage scales and craft agreements patterned after those of the oldest urban properties.

We suspect that personnel development, laddered promotion, and merit pay increases are a prerequisite of transit stabilization, but this cannot be asserted with certainty. What can be stated with certainty is that no conventional strategy for restraining the growth of unit labor costs has proved effective in the past 30 years.

Achieving Sustained Productivity Improvement

There are numerous opportunities to achieve modest improvements in the productivity of urban transit systems. Examples include wider use of part-time labor, more efficient use of idle labor and equipment, traffic engineering measures that increase the efficiency of operations in mixed traffic, and measures that "spread the peak"—measures such as staggered or flexible working hours. These are one-time improvements that can produce marginal gains in operational productivity and financial performance. Implemented in combination or in series, they might afford the opportunity to increase the industry's productivity by as much as 10 percent and net revenues by a comparably small fraction. But we cannot look to these measures to provide the kind of sustained productivity improvement and revenue growth necessary to offset the growth of unit operating costs. The measures mentioned are susceptible to early exhaustion and thus have only temporary value. More troubling is the danger that we will mistake palliatives for substantive action and use them as an excuse to defer real change. More troubling still is that it is almost impossible to imagine productivity improvements that would have more than temporary or palliative value. This is the dilemma that has confounded transit management since the 1920s.

The industry has responded to this central dilemma with the argument that transit is a social service that should not be expected to pay for itself entirely from the farebox. We agree with this conclusion, but we cannot agree that the general taxpayer should be expected to pay more and more for a social service of declining quality. Redefining transit as a social service does not resolve the industry's productivity problem; it simply reminds us to specify that this is a *service* industry with a grave productivity problem.

How can the productivity problem be resolved if we cannot imagine a strategy for achieving sustained improvement? This is the crux of the matter and the question that has gone unanswered for six decades.

PRODUCTIVITY IMPROVEMENT AND STRUCTURAL CHANGE

The transit industry's productivity problem is rooted in structural dead-lock; it is a problem that cannot be resolved without structural change. Management cannot obtain labor cooperation for productivity improvement because the industry's wage structure does not reward increasing productivity. Management cannot increase productivity by capturing off-peak ridership because its fleet mix and route structure are designed to serve the peak. The industry cannot increase fares at the pace necessary to offset cost escalation because its fare structure is perversely rigged to discourage patronage by short-distance and off-peak trip makers; thus fares cannot be increased without further damaging productivity. Nor is it possible to raise peak-hour fares to recover marginal costs because transit's primary competitor, the automobile, is subsidized or, more precisely, because the auto used for urban commuting is advantaged by intertemporal cross-subsidies and privileged arrangements for parking.

If these compound constraints could be relaxed, sustained productivity improvement *might* be feasible, at least in some urban markets. Table 10-3 itemizes the six major elements of the compound change

TABLE 10-3 An Agenda for Structural Change

A new fare structure	One that is differentiated by time of day and distance traveled
Greater discretion to price service in relation to cost	Achievable if a surtax is imposed on all-day parking
A new sales-oriented organization structure	One that is decentralized so that planning, routing, and scheduling decisions can be based on an intimate knowledge of the market for locally customized services
A different fleet mix	One with the capacity necessary to serve the peak but better suited to shuttle, charter, and taxilike operations in the off-peak
A wider diversity of service offerings	Some sold on a contract or subscription basis, some purchased from private vendors
A new contract with labor	One that permits wider use of part-time and cross-trained employees while creating a wider range of promotion opportunities for transit workers

strategy we believe is necessary to position transit to achieve sustained productivity improvement. The actions needed to renew transit include (1) peak-hour pricing linked to a surtax on automobile parking, (2) a new contract with labor that permits wider use of part-time and cross-trained employees, (3) a vehicle fleet that is better suited to productive operation in the off-peak, and (4) a wider diversity of service offerings matched by a new sales-oriented organization structure. We recognize that change of this magnitude is unlikely in the extreme, given its controversiality and the effective veto power that can be exercised by influential urban constituencies. Individual elements of the agenda are susceptible to implementation, but no transit property could orchestrate the implementation of our compound change strategy in its entirety. However, *compound* change is needed to create the pricing discretion and catalyze the organizational change, technological innovation, and enterprising management the transit industry lacks. The tragedy is that such change is unlikely to be achieved.

THE MERITS OF STRUCTURAL CHANGE

Conceding that compound change is unlikely and impolitic does not abrogate our obligation to explain why it would be worth doing could it be done. We must discuss the merits of the case, regardless of its political feasibility.

Our agenda for structural change included six major elements—elements that are linked and paired in compound fashion. We will consider each cluster of strategies in turn.

Differential Pricing and a Parking Surtax

Transit's current fare structure bears little relation to the cost of providing peak-hour service or serving trips of any considerable length. Flat fares overprice short-distance and off-peak travel and underprice long-distance and peak-hour travel. Peak-hour auto travel is underpriced in much the same fashion, due in large measure to "free" parking. Close to 90 percent of the American workforce park free at their place of work, and only a fraction of those who pay to park pay rates that are unsubsidized. "Free" parking is far from costless. Indeed, the result is a classic "tragedy of the commons." "Free" parking results in excessive consumption of peak-hour roadspace and in automotive pollution levels much greater than those which would result if parking were rationed by price. "Free" parking also goes a long way to explain the inability of transit properties to price rush-hour service in a fashion that approximates the marginal cost of serving the peak. The result is a fare structure that impairs transit's earning power and aggravates the imbalance of peak and off-peak traffic.

This is a compound problem that requires a compound resolution. The economics of both peaking and pollution argue for replacing transit's current sources of local tax support—most often property taxes, sales taxes, or payroll taxes—with revenues derived from an areawide surtax on parking. A parking tax would function as a proxy for the congestion tolls which economists have long argued are necessary to price peak-hour auto use in relation to marginal cost. It would reduce automotive pollution while permitting transit to introduce the fare structure necessary to recoup ridership in the short-distance and off-peak markets.

A Wider Diversity of Service Offerings, a Different Fleet Mix, and a New Sales-Oriented Organizational Structure

Most transit properties offer standardized service with standardized equipment. Fixed route, fixed schedule service afforded by a fleet composed almost exclusively of 55-passenger buses is the industry norm. This fleet and its method of operation suits the peak, but it is mismatched with the latent demand for public transportation in the off-peak. It is a fleet that can only clumsily be used in charter, shuttle, and off-boulevard operation.

Thus, we argue for gradual fleet retirement and the replacement of the standard 55-passenger bus with a mixed fleet of high-capacity articulated buses, luxury express coaches, and microbuses of light weight and low noise suited to off-boulevard door-to-door service in the off-peak. Such a mix of vehicles could provide peak-hour capacity equivalent to that afforded by an homogenous fleet of 55-passenger buses— but it would be much better suited to charter and demand-responsive operation in the off-peak.

Fleet change would be purposeless without a corresponding change in the transit industry's organization structure. A more diverse fleet could not be used effectively unless transit managers develop a tactile feel for local markets and for segments of the off-peak market that are poorly served by both conventional transit and the automobile. A community-based, geographically decentralized approach to planning, marketing, routing and salesmanship is necessary to enter these markets with operations customized to serve latent demand.

The merit of entering such markets is twofold. They afford an opportunity to use labor and equipment that would otherwise remain idle during the midday. And, as important, it is in such markets that transit could truly perform an essential service role for the elderly, handicapped, and those who are carless.

A New Contract with Labor

Unless labor productivity is steadily increased, wage gains realized by transit workers will continue to erode the industry's financial position. Increases in productivity can be obtained by wider use of permanent part-time employees and cross-trained workers who perform hyphenated work assignments such as driver-mechanic and driver-accountant. Productivity can also be increased by using labor in off-peak driving assignments associated with a wider diversity of services.

Thus, the key to achieving productivity gain is not more work for less pay, but wage scales, training programs and career ladders that reward transit workers for advancing to job roles that are increasingly productive. With a merit-based promotion system, transit workers could better their standard of living without base-wage increases that exceed cost of living adjustment.

Such are the merits of compound structural change. The demerit of structural change is of a different sort: it would abrogate entitlements vested by custom and tradition, provoking the resistance of organized urban constituencies. In the absence of countervailing constituency support for change, it appears all too likely that the gradual erosion and attrition of transit service will continue. This is not a happy prognosis, but it is transit's most probable path into the future. We have reached the heart of the matter and, like transit management, we seem to be stymied by political stalemate and structural deadlock.

Nonetheless, we have at least arrived at a reasonably complete specification of the transit stabilization problem. Stabilizing mass transit is a compound institutional, technological, and economic problem characterized by structural deadlock and political stalemate. The challenge is to break that deadlock without abrogating the economic rights of transit workers and without sacrificing reasonable continuity of service and fares.

Our analysis of transit's relations with local government persuades us that this is a deadlock that cannot be resolved—at least in the first instance—through local initiative. Structural change cannot be proposed by local officialdom or instigated at their behest. It would simply entail too much controversy and too much political risk.

We are left with one resort: the active and constructive involvement of the federal government in a role that simultaneously fosters change and buffers its adverse impacts.

THE FEDERAL ROLE IN TRANSIT STABILIZATION

There are numerous precedents for federal involvement in industrial reorganization. The most recent examples are the reorganization of the Chrysler Corporation and the transformation of the Penn Central into

Conrail. In both instances, the federal government provided the financial wherewithal for reorganization and the third-party good offices necessary to revise entitlements equitably. The requisites of transit stabilization are analogous: stabilization will require compound structural change, the revision of entitlements, and financial assistance. Financial assistance is needed to buffer the effects of change and, as important, to motivate labor, management, and local officialdom to venture change. Here, however, the analogy ends. Unlike Conrail and the Chrysler Corporation, mass transit is a fragmented and localized service industry. Each transit property is managerially idiosyncratic and each market served is essentially unique. Structural obsolescence is an industrywide phenomenon, but the appropriate remedy will vary in balance, proportion, and composition from locality to locality. So will the locality's social and political tolerance for change.

The challenge then is to construct a stabilization and reorganization program that motivates localities to venture change, but that does so permissively rather than either preemptively or prescriptively. Federal intervention must enhance management's discretion by increasing its options; it must not preempt local initiative or prescribe performance standards that inhibit unique local remedies to unique local problems.

A carefully crafted program of conditional subsidy would satisfy this specification. A conditional subsidy program might be built around a transit merit fund. Merit fund revenues would be reserved for those properties that qualify for additional financial assistance by meeting certain broadly stated conditions. Additional subsidies would be provided to transit properties that can certify that they have:

1. Introduced differential fares for peak and off-peak service
2. Negotiated a labor contract which permits the use of part-time operators and permits cross-training and hyphenated work assignments
3. Adopted an operations, marketing, and resource management plan for midday and weekend service.

As we have postulated its architecture this would be a broadly permissive program. Local officials would have the clear option of nonparticipation. Local discretion would also govern the extent of fare differentiation, the extent of off-peak service differentiation and the extent to which part-time and cross-trained employees are actually used.

Qualifying for additional subsidy from the Transit Merit Fund would be much less difficult and controversial than a locally-instigated effort to implement the agenda for stabilization proposed in Table

10-3. One reason is obvious: the federal initiative that we propose is far less ambitious than our full agenda for structural change. It does not include, for example, a parking tax, nor does it oblige transit properties to decentralize planning and management authority. This is intentional. The federal initiative we propose is conceived as a modest but *achievable* first step in the direction of structural change.

The cautiously conceived changes we have proposed as conditions of subsidy are not, in themselves, sufficient to produce sustained productivity improvement or a stable transit industry. They are just what we have described them: modest first steps. They are steps on a path that leads toward reorganization, but only halting first steps.

As modest as the changes proposed may be, it is unlikely they would be made in the absence of the incentive created by additional federal subsidy. Federal involvement is the key to their implementation because additional federal aid would buffer the short-run dislocation that is inherent in any strategy of structural change. Two examples will illustrate this point. With federal subsidy a transit property could achieve fare differentiation by reducing off-peak fares—a far less controversial step than imposing a peak-hour surcharge, but one which would produce a fare structure of identical architecture. The incremental subsidy received from the national treasury would off-set the revenue loss resulting from off-peak fare reduction. While passenger revenues would decline over the short run, the property would now be positioned with a fare structure that minimizes the ridership loss occasioned by future fare increases.

The conflict associated with contract provisions permitting the use of part-time and cross-trained workers could be dampened in a similar fashion. Additional subsidy would permit the property to hire such workers without displacing present jobholders.

As these examples suggest, the merit of carefully crafted federal involvement is that it would transform a game with winners and losers into a win-win situation. It represents, then, a strategy for revising vested entitlements and initiating structural change without breaching the social contract among transit properties, their workforce, and the communities they serve. The intent is to achieve that initial breakthrough necessary to dissolve transit's structural deadlock. Breaking that deadlock represents the beginning—not the end—of a long and difficult process. It is a beginning that will lead nowhere in many cities and regions. But in a select few cities it may galvanize a process that leads to the reorganization, entrepreneurial management, and technological innovation necessary for sustained productivity improvement. It is on the performance of a few innovators in a few cities that we pin our hopes. Where they lead, others will follow. This is the merit of constructive federal involvement in the reorganization and renewal of mass transit. The case rests on creating a unique opportunity for innovative management to venture change.

CLOSURE

This book began with the observation that mass transit is both a distressed industry and an essential social service. We have focused on the industry's financial distress because it has compromised transit's performance as a social service. Even with federal, state, and local subsidy, transit properties continue to experience periodic financial crises that jeopardize their ability to function as a reliable public service.

The subsidy programs shaped in the 1960s and 1970s were designed to preserve service, stabilize fares and protect job rights rather than detonate a process of organizational change and renewal. This was their shortcoming. Without reorganization, more and more subsidy was required to preserve service and stabilize ridership. Subsidy provided a reprieve for transit but it did not resolve the industry's long-standing financial problems. That reprieve proved short-lasting. A recovery based on steadily increasing subsidy could not be sustained, and ridership declined again with the leveling off of subsidy payments in the 1980s.

A different kind of subsidy program might have produced different results—a program conceived as an instrument of change rather than preservation. Change in the organization of transit service is needed because the industry's form and function no longer match. Transit's form dates to the era before World War I when the street railway was the dominant mode of urban transportation. The industry's fare structure, service mix, routing philosophy, and labor contracts reflect the functions that it performed and the markets that it served in the era prior to automotive competition. Since then, the growth of automobile ownership and use has eroded transit's ridership selectively, destroying the balance of peak and off-peak ridership and the density of traffic necessary for efficient operation. The diffusion of the automobile fundamentally changed transit's function. Transit became a subordinate and supplemental form of urban transportation, dominant in only one market—travel to and from work in the central cities of the nation's oldest industrial and commercial centers. Little change in form accompanied this fundamental change in function. Private ownership yielded to public ownership and electric traction to the diesel motorbus, but these represent relatively superficial adjustments. Much more basic change would have been necessary to restore consonance of form and function.

Matching form and function can still be accomplished but it would require compound change: change in the industry's fare structure and service mix; change in its organizational format and fleet mix; and change in its labor agreements and use of personnel. As this itemization suggests, compound, not incremental, change would be necessary to match services and markets, form and function.

Transit management has been understandably reluctant to venture such fundamental change. A handful of innovative managers have broached the issue, calling for "a bold new approach to an old problem," but risk-aversion has prevailed as the industry norm. No property has ventured compound change because both the risk and resistance would be enormous.

In the absence of fundamental change, gradual economic attrition will characterize the industry's future—as it has its past. This is an unhappy but realistic prognosis. It is a prognosis that argues for a carefully crafted federal initiative which creates incentive for change—while sharing its risk and buffering its impact. To date, federal transit policy has emphasized the preservation rather than the reorganization of service. Preservation without reorganization is insufficient. For transit, change is the essence of stabilization.

INDEX